FRANKENSTEIN'S MANAGER

FRANKENSTEIN'S MANAGER

———✡———

Leadership's Missing Links

Bill McAneny

Oak Tree Press

Dublin

Oak Tree Press
Merrion Building
Lower Merrion Street
Dublin 2, Ireland
http://www.oaktreepress.com

© 2000 Bill McAneny

ISBN 1 86076 149 6

Printed in Britain by MPG Books,
Bodmin, Cornwall

Contents

About the Author

Bill McAneny is an organisational psychologist based in London. His company, Prelude Consulting Limited, is primarily involved in organisational and leadership development. As well as his consulting work, Bill teaches psychology to senior executives from all over the world at the International Management Academies in Brussels and Stockholm, set up by the Swedish Institute of Management. He also speaks at conferences on a range of business, psychology, organisational and development topics.

Acknowledgements

Thanks to Karen Loring for all her help, support, ideas and pedantry.

This book is dedicated to:

Denise Elizabeth McAneny
Claire Elizabeth McAneny
David McAneny
Ellen McAneny

Introduction

You remember the old joke, "what's black and white and read all over?" Well, the answer is certainly not books on leadership. Very few are "black and white", and even fewer are "read all over". At best, they are dipped into for the odd quotable morsel; at worst, they gather dust among all the other guru books, like a mausoleum of leadership theory — "yesterday's papers telling yesterday's news", as they say.

Most leadership books are bought on impulse, often with the view that, "this one may hold all the answers". Once the introduction has been flicked through, the first chapter half-read, and a quick glance at the end to see "whodunnit", it is placed on the shelf with the promise that, "I will come back to it tomorrow". But tomorrow is another day, another guru! Leadership books are the sort of books that, once you put them down, you can't pick them up again! I have been in the offices of some awfully senior executives, and a quick sniff through the bookshelves tells me all I need to know; a horror story for publishers — "the night of the unread"!

I wanted to write a book that may actually be useful. Oh, I know we all say that. But I'd like to challenge the way managers think — about business, about leadership, about people, about themselves. Maybe it is a little controversial, suggesting that the usual "management skills" training is not the answer in creating better performing leaders (though to be honest, I think we all know this anyway); but it does seem to me to be common sense. Most of all, I wanted to write a book that will make YOU better at what you do for a living, what you get paid for: leading people. Not by cramming your head full of the latest theories and "guru-speak", but by helping you make some sense of your basic, and most precious, resources — your people — and developing the leader that is already in you. There is no one right way to lead, only your way, with all your foibles and idiosyncrasies.

The basic premise of this book is that "management skills" training does not work, does not lead to better-performing managers. I spoke with the managing director of a leading UK training provider who told me that "85 per cent of our management courses are a waste of time". Now, he was not necessarily rubbishing his own courses, simply being practical and realistic about the outputs — what happens *after* management training. There are just too many variables affecting a leader's performance that a "skills" training course could not hope to address. The menu, or wish list, of "management skills" training on offer by training providers channels leadership down a single route and, in seeking competency, we create mediocrity; we create Dolly, the managerial sheep.

In one of the UK tabloids some years ago, they decided to make a composite of "the perfect woman". They put together what they considered were all the "best bits" from women generally acclaimed to be beautiful at that time. The results were . . . well, awful! The "perfect" woman looked like Frankenstein's monster. By taking only pieces from other people, we lose the very essence of what made these people special: their completeness, together with all their strange, quirky bits.

In many respects, this is what happens with leadership training. The course begins with the facilitator getting participants to identify who the great leaders are, both historical and modern, and then brainstorming to decide upon the common denominators, the shared characteristics which make or made them "great".

This theory, like all of us as individuals, is basically flawed. If we cut Richard Branson in half, we would not have two Richard Bransons; we would have a dead Richard Branson. The essence of what he is comes from all the components, positive and negative, which form his character.

Such courses use people like Richard Branson, Winston Churchill, Mahatma Gandhi, John F. Kennedy as examples of great leaders. Yet when we begin to explore the characteristics, we get contradictory information: tall versus short, charismatic versus pragmatic, aggressive versus conciliatory, etc., etc. The key here is for all of us to recognise that there is no magic formula for making perfect leaders, just as we cannot create the perfect woman or man. So let's forget the idea of a perfect leader or a perfect management/leadership training programme. We do not attend "Friendship Skills" programmes, and yet we each manage to make, and keep, close friends.

Great leadership comes from within, from understanding ourselves and others. Trying to artificially create the perfect leader draws us towards creating Frankenstein's monster, an unnatural amalgam of disparate parts which do not belong together.

The better leaders with whom I have worked transcend "skills", "techniques" and "competency". For example, leaders who habitually don't listen are often encouraged to attend a "listening skills" course. What is this all about? The more enlightened leaders really do listen because they are interested and want to hear what people are saying. Yet, when attending the programme, these non-listening leaders are often taught how to *pretend to listen*. You know, how to make their eyes big, maintain eye contact, nod in all the right places, say "mm hmm" at strategic points in the conversation. They learn how to replay and paraphrase: "I see, so what you are saying is . . ." In short, they can learn how to convince the other person that they are listening without actually hearing a word!

Our own use of language often channels the way we attempt to develop our leaders. If someone is habitually late for meetings, it is said that they have a "time management problem". No, they don't! They are simply habitually late for meetings. Yet, by our use of language, we are determining the outcome before analysing the issue — going for the easy option. This ignores the fact that the person may be superfluous to the meeting (or even, heaven forbid, that the meeting itself is superfluous!) So, the person attends the "time management skills" course, comes back fully conversant with the theories and knowledge of time management, armed with a plastic filofax — and is still habitually late for meetings!

"Communication skills" is another old chestnut, a box into which we can place any leader who doesn't let people know what is going on. How often do we hear that someone lacks "communication skills?" It's probably the second most common charge levelled at leaders in organisations, after "people skills". So what should they do? Attend a "communication skills" course! Maybe they can learn Morse code and semaphore! Communication is a desire, not a skill. If we feel it is important that people be kept informed, then we will keep them informed. OK, so some aspects of a presentation may need brushing up on, but even "presentation skills" implies a "one right way", and I don't believe there is. In fact, presentations are often not the best way to keep people informed, either for the audience or the person delivering the message. An introvert is unlikely to be able to communicate in the same way as an extrovert, but that does not mean that each cannot get their message across as effectively. (The terms "introvert" and "extrovert" are discussed later in this book. The pop psychology definitions of "boring" versus "popular" are not what Jung intended!)

In 2000, one of the most popular training courses (and myths) on offer is "How to Manage Change". As the existentialist philosopher Søren Kierkegaard said, "life is best understood backwards, but it has to be lived forwards". If we accept this, how can we "manage" change? Many events will happen over which we have no control or forewarning; how can we claim to be able to "manage" them? All we can do is learn to manage our responses to change and, more importantly, help those we lead manage their responses. Just as financial planners beaver away to produce a three-month forecast and then, three months down the line, put together a rationalisation of why it didn't happen the way they said it would, so the idea that we might be able to "manage" change may give us delusions of control!

Leadership development will happen through behavioural modification. Understanding ourselves and the impact of our behaviour is the starting point for the process of bringing out and developing the leader in each of us. But it is only the starting point.

We cannot change our personalities, but we can, if we *choose*, modify our behaviour. Just as behaviour is choice, so too is development. In my experience, "management skills" training does not provide lasting behavioural modification in individuals or any lasting improvement in performance. It is all too easy to see leadership as a series of "skills" rather than intrinsically our own behaviour. From the perspective of a training provider, or even a HR manager, this makes sense. Having a menu (or wish list) of "management skills" or "competencies" makes it easier to sell the concept of "management training", breaking "leadership" down into a collection of easy-to-digest, bite-sized chunks. Yet so often, several weeks down the line, that those who participated recollect a few tasty morsels, regurgitate some of Maslow's well-chewed ideas, and recall how good the beer was at the hotel and how the trainer had "the scars"!

"Skills training" is not a long-term (or, to be honest, even a short-term) answer. Environment played a major part in forming who we are, and our environment still plays a big part in our day-to-day lives. We all know this, and yet we still expect our people to attend courses and come back with their behaviour modified to such an extent that they as individuals will be transformed for life. As Woody Allen said, "meanwhile, back on the planet Earth!"

Modifying behaviour does not mean trying to be something we are not. It simply means that, having understood the impact of our behaviour, we choose to change. This is the starting point for personal development. There are an exponential number of fresh, innovative and interesting ways for leaders to develop without reaching for the training prospectus.

OK, so the journey may not be straightforward, and certainly not easy, but the 1,000-mile march begins with the first step.

"Training" is a passive term. The active term is "development", which occurs *after* training or, more often, *without it*! It is all too easy (but very expensive) to see training as the answer to leadership problems. What we all need is not so much training, as to go through an "unlearning" process, to rid ourselves of our very human desire to form perceptions and make judgements of others. Leadership is a people game, and a contact sport. There are no expert leaders, just as there are no expert friends, or husbands, or wives.

The Latin root of the word "education" is *educere*, meaning "leading out". In the same way, rather than trying to cram the heads of leaders full of the latest theories, we can create the conditions where we can develop the individual leader in each person. The ultimate aim for all leaders is to take responsibility for their own development. Not for booking them- selves on the latest course, but accepting that devel- opment will happen in many different ways, and learning to maximise their own opportunities for learning, which is the key to continuous, transforma- tional, development.

Too many HR managers accept the *concept* of self- development as a way of moving the responsibility for leadership development away from the HR func- tion towards each individual leader. Ultimately, this is the right way to go. However, for leaders used to having a menu of courses from which to choose, who believe development is about attending courses, the move to behavioural-based development can be a bit of a culture shock. So leaders will need guidance in the early days to establish their own most appropriate ways of learning and to create fresh ways to develop themselves and the people they lead.

This book is written primarily for leaders, but also for HR professionals, for consultants, for anyone who is interested in effecting lasting, memorable, transformational, continuous development in themselves, in the people they lead, in the people they serve. It is *not* written for those who want the latest fad, those who see "management training" as something *done to* them, or those who want a quick fix. Development is like walking towards the horizon; we never actually get there. But, if every so often, we look back, we can see just how far we have come.

I do focus on some core leadership issues such as "the leader as teacher", "the leader as designer", "creating magnetic north", the "customer-centred leader", and "the leader in each of us". But mostly, the book focuses on you, and what you can do to be better at what you get paid for. No matter what your starting point. It is unashamedly people-centred, because that is what leadership is all about.

In this book, I explore and simplify many of the complexities of leadership and explain why "management training" is not the answer. I also identify a variety of ways in which we can bring out the best in developing leaders, from within. Rather than trying to artificially create something, why not make the best of what we already have, bringing out the leader in each of us? We can learn to understand ourselves and the impact of our behaviour, positive and negative! Then we can work with our own unique characteristics to develop further. There really can be creative, unique, fresh ways of moving forward and becoming much better at what we do. Limiting ourselves to a stale "management skills menu" or "wish-list" (which is often what it is) severely restricts our capacity to achieve quantum leaps in self-development.

The book takes as its theme the idea that "management skills" training tries to create leaders artificially, and draws an analogy with Frankenstein's monster. We often try to create the perfect leader by stitching together worn-out ideas, threadbare theories and the ragbag of experiences of other people, rather than looking afresh at ourselves as individuals, understanding the impact of our behaviour, developing from within. This book will help you achieve this.

Do I expect it to be "read all over"? I'd love to think so, but then reality bites! So feel free to dip in and around the book. Perhaps begin, as we all tend to do, by dipping into the middle, or near the end, read a paragraph and see if it inspires you. This is the usual buying criterion for business books. I hope you find it interesting, illuminating, energising and FRESH. If not, let me know. If you do, I'd still be pleased to hear from you (bill@prelude-team.com).

Part 1

Dispelling the Myths of Management

Whisper it quietly: "There is no magic formula for the perfect leader". The "myths" that follow are all related to the one big myth: the myth that there is a recipe for the "Perfect Leader" out there, waiting to be grafted onto you, if only you could find the correct ingredients. It's time to dispel those myths.

THE "TRAINING IS THE SOLUTION" MYTH

With the resurgence of training budgets in the late 1990s, there has been a strong focus on "developing management skills". Courses such as "The High Performance Leader", "Action-Centred Leadership" and (the less buzzy) "The Effective Leader" abound in the business press, as do endless articles, tracts and books on the subject. There is little evidence of better performance as a result; just more managers aware of the buzzwords and more training companies flogging their wares.

The usual cry of anguish when problems arise in any organisation is, "we need more training". But training is not the answer. Our environment and experiences create who we are as people and leaders, and there are an exponential number of variables, day-by-day, week-by-week, affecting our performance. Yet we often expect a single event such as a training course to have earth-shattering results in terms of behavioural modification. This is not a realistic expectation.

It seems so obvious to me that changes in their out-of-hours life (say, a reduction in their overdraft, going through a divorce, impending marriage, having kids, etc.) may have a much greater impact on a person's behaviour, and so a greater effect upon their overall performance at work.

Sure, we get a bit of a buzz after the course, and participants often come back fired up and ready to try to do things differently. Yet what they often face are the same problems they faced before they attended the course: an unchanged environment and a week's backlog of work in the in-tray resulting from their "week away". Indeed, I have often seen training courses create such expectation in individuals that, several weeks or months down the line, they feel worse than they did before they attended the programme. People often don't just "go back to square one"; they often go below it. Perhaps courses should include a section on managing expectations!

Trainers too know how to "use" the buzz factor. I have attended courses where, at 3.45 on the final day of the programme, the trainer recognises that energy levels are depleting and brings in a couple of "energisers" (games or activities designed to get everyone in the group moving again), thus boosting the energy levels, ahead of dishing out the "how useful has this course been?" evaluation forms. As these are completed when participants are on a "high", we tend to get artificially high "readings", reflecting how individuals were feeling at the time of scoring, rather than how effective the learning has been, and how useful the outputs will be. Completing the evaluation six weeks down the line, at 6.00 p.m. in the middle of a busy factory, would probably be a better gauge.

Now this book is not "anti-trainer". It is not a question of "blame" or "fault". Many organisations, and leaders themselves, are looking for a "quick fix", and rather than spend the time on nurturing leaders, many would prefer to spend the money with a training provider, dated, signed, box ticked: *I have been trained!* Such organisations also often believe that the more money they spend on the course, going for the more prestigious institutions, the better "trained" their people will be. Again, this is placing far too great an emphasis on the training establishment and far too little on the individual leader as learner.

Training versus Learning

As I said earlier, we need to undergo an "unlearning process" to get out of the bad habit of forcing our behaviour and judgements on others without looking at the facts or consequences. We begin to become better as leaders only through understanding ourselves and others (the basic raw materials in leadership). No chemist would be let loose on creating compounds or mixing a cocktail of chemicals without fully understanding all the ingredients. Yet as leaders we are expected to build teams, make selection and promotion decisions, manage careers, etc. without having an in-depth knowledge of our basic raw materials.

The distinction I drew earlier between "training" and "development" is more than a distinction of syntax, as it places far greater emphasis on the person who is being developed, and on the provider to create the right conditions where learning can take place. It is also a recognition of the variety of methods through which different people learn.

"Management training", as I have experienced it, often seeks to clone managers, to make all managers alike as it focuses on "core skills", or "competencies" (which sounds to me like "mediocrity"). People are far more complex than that. At a more practical level, skills training may serve to compartmentalise the role of a manager and so narrow the remit.

Conversely, if part of the "management skills" course is, for example, "coaching and counselling skills", some managers may believe their responsibilities have been extended and they now have something else to take on, "more stuff dumped on me". Part of any development process must be to focus on the people issues and let each individual begin to understand the role of leader and what it means to them.

Putting "management skills" into a box may be useful for training providers to sell their wares, or for human resources people to "sell" training packages to line managers. However, it may also reduce the ability of thinking, feeling individuals to understand the wider picture and put their own individual stamp on situations.

Learning about ourselves and about other people will allow us the facility to deal better with people issues and situations and so become better managers. Managing our own perceptions and prejudices is the key to a real understanding.

THE "COMPETENCY" MYTH

The word "competent" has been overused in business parlance for a long time. The idea behind developing "competencies" was to find the magic point
at which individuals knew they were "fit for purpose", like an ISO 9000 procedure. I brought in a
specialist pressure vessel design engineer to one of
our customers. I took up a reference on him from a
professor of vessel design at a top European University. "How would you describe him?" I asked. "I can
pay him no higher compliment than to say he is . . ." I
couldn't wait: what's the highest compliment the top
vessel professor in the world can pay you? ". . . competent!" Well, that fell a bit flat. I pushed slightly, and
asked if he could maybe elaborate. "We live in a
world of soap powder commercials, of words like
'wonderful' and 'fabulous'. To an engineer, 'competent' is the highest compliment we can have be-
stowed upon us." It certainly made me think.

Not only does the word "competent" smack of
minimum standard, and mediocrity, it conjures up
images of the "one way" of leading people, and I
can't subscribe to this. Also, at a slightly more philo-
sophical level, the term was designed to be absolute,
a gatepost where we all fall one side or the other. We
are either "competent" or "incompetent". Now, I
don't hear many leaders being described during
their appraisal as "incompetent". What I do hear are
terms like "very competent", "quite competent",
"really competent", "extremely competent", "really,

really competent"! And the worst one of all, in a local authority, "not yet competent"! Imagine how he felt?

Prior to 1980, children in the United Kingdom with special needs were termed "educationally subnormal"; horrible, isn't it? Educational psychologists, (affectionately known in the trade as "Ed Psychs"), would measure a youngster and, depending on where they were pinpointed on the normal distribution curve, they were either labelled "normal", or "subnormal". Those children who were on the wrong side of the gatepost were deemed subnormal. A few percentile points up and they could have fallen into the normal band and been "saved".

Mary Warnock changed the terminology to "special needs". Now this was not simply an attempt to find a term that was less horrific than "subnormal", but a whole change of mind-set. Her report suggested that, rather than a "pass or fail" gatepost, we are all on the same continuum. We all have needs and each of us, at particular times in our lives, might have special needs. Therefore, the focus is to keep developing and moving forward, accepting that we will, at times, backslide and need help.

In the same way, leadership development is not a gatepost. It is a continuum: we are all on it, and we all move forward and occasionally slide back. This is called being human. So to use terms like "competent" fudges a complex and individual issue and, whilst it might be a useful "tick box" exercise for HR managers, I don't think it furthers the cause of leadership development.

In trying to find a formula for perfection in management, many of those on the receiving end are becoming confused, bemused and weighed down. Many training providers may believe they have found "the formula" in the menus they compile of "management skills". Yet, in the cold light of an early business morning, have they become better leaders as perceived by the people they lead? I have actually heard some leaders complain that this is an unfair way to judge the success of a training programme! My argument is: what other way is there?

THE "CHANGE MANAGEMENT" MYTH

Change is in vogue. But what exactly is meant by "managing change"? It almost implies that we can give leaders the power of divination, a sort of "Mystic Meg Management Programme", as though we can have complete control over what happens in the future! Things will happen in life over which we have no control or prior warning. The key, rather, is for leaders to learn to manage their *responses* to change, rather than futilely trying to halt the inevitable, or predict the future.

Like all leadership principles and challenges, change is a people issue. Telling people that change is inevitable and drawing on the laws of nature will not help someone who is genuinely afraid of change. Beating them around the head with Handy's *The Empty Raincoat* will never be as beneficial as getting to know each as an individual and helping to lead them towards being better placed to respond positively to new initiatives and change.

Even those who claim to be advocates of change, or "change agents", worry me for a different reason. I took the main board of a major worldwide engineering group for a session on "understanding people". When I arrived, they were not happy. They were 17 of the most senior people from one of the largest and most successful organisations in the world, and they did not want me, a psychologist, to work with them. "We are a very successful organisation." "We live and breathe change every day, what could you possibly teach us?" These were some of the comments.

I began the session with a bit of a jolt: I issued each of them with a notice of redundancy. This did not go down well at all! There were many complaints, and some ranting. A few of the more astute within the group noticed that the memo was dated 31 December 2000. The brief I gave them was to look back on today (4 January 1999), reflect, and tell me why they were all sacked. What did they not do which they should have, what did they do which they shouldn't have? This is a very gentle introduction to get senior people owning up to their weaknesses and areas where they need to start doing things differently, but within a "safe" environment.

Whilst they were out of the room, I changed the seating around. This was no psychological ploy; simply that I don't like a classroom style when I'm working. When the group returned an hour later, they didn't know where to sit; they wandered around in a daze, blamed each other and asked me to tell them where to sit. What struck me about these "agents of change" was that when they say "we love change", they were actually saying, "we love changing things". They like change when it is something they do, not when it is something which is done to them.

It is a bit like the difference between buying things and being sold to. We all tend to like buying, because it is our choice. But being sold to is like being told what to do, and we resist. Through this accident of changed seating, I was able to get them to face up to the realities of change and so move them forward in their understanding of people.

Begin by looking in the mirror

A major underlying fear about change is the fact that "scientific" reasons are not going to help. An increase in sales, a market turnaround, new investment, etc., may happen, but these are not the primary issues. The main fear is the fact that the people themselves, *as individuals*, will have to change.

So often when I am invited to work with businesses, management are seeking impersonal solutions to their problems — new technology, structural changes, process solutions — when all the time the answers are right there in front of their noses, staring them in the face every time they look in the mirror.

Management is not an exact science and does not conform to a set of scientific laws. However, neither is it something only the clever can grasp. The best we can hope for is a set of ground-rules, some of which will not fit with our character, some of which will seem common-sense, and some ideas we can use and which fit with us as people. We can buy books on "Change Management" or "Empowerment" and read what other people have done and what works for them. This may help, or may make you feel like an abject failure.

Instead, look in the mirror, because that is where the change process starts, for you, for your team and for your organisation. Painful, isn't it?

"But we don't want to keep reinventing the wheel"

Oh yeah? How many cars run on stone wheels? How many cars run on 1950s-style wheels with white wall tyres? Everything keeps moving forward, and we are glad they do. Despite this, leaders often apply the same principles that got them in the trouble they are in today — but apply them harder!

One of the great paradoxes I find in my work is that the companies which most need help are the ones which benefit least, much like patients requiring therapy. Leaders of poorly performing companies tend to shun advice and believe the same old ways of working, the same old formulas, just applied harder, will provide all the answers. Such leaders, in my experience, see "change" as a personal attack or a threat to them as individuals, rather than as a way of improving business performance.

The senior teams appear to be more adverse to change than middle-level managers who will, ultimately, go with the flow. I know this goes against the "accepted wisdom" that middle-level managers are usually the stumbling blocks, the "sponge in the middle", but I don't buy that. When it comes to accepting the fact that it is they who must change, that the "change management programme" is not the answer, then I have seen leaders at all levels get jittery.

One of the most interesting issues we find in our work is discovering why managers themselves will not change, why they fail to face up to the necessity and inevitability of change. We have found so many managers who have been "in the job" 23 years but don't have 23 years' experience. They have one year's experience 23 times, and will continue in this loop until they retire or expire. Yet "seniority" is often valued more highly than added value. "What if we lose all that experience?" It is an assumption that "the elders" possess some sort of magical wisdom; that, like some sort of totem pole, will cause the business to fail if it is removed. If leaders in organisations really believe this, then perhaps they should be spending more time "divining" all this knowledge out of "the elders", rather than hoping against hope that they will not leave. Now, I am not in any way being "ageist"; I have worked with many old 20-year-olds and very young 70-year-olds! This issue is more about the processes organisations set up to gather and harness knowledge, rather than "Should Fred or Freda be retained for another year, 'just in case'?"

Also, senior managers often believe they "got where they are today" by operating within a particular set of rules and values and so have a vested interest in the status quo.

The internal antibodies that fight change

In organisations where I have been tasked with major change processes, such managers often work insidiously, rarely coming out and voicing opposition, but working behind the scenes to undermine the change process and "rubbish" the work that is taking place. Rather than embrace wholesale change, many senior managers often want to begin the process in smaller, "non-vital" areas of the company; such as in the sales order processing function or in the warehouse. This always worries me. Also, the areas recommended as "starting points" often tell us more about the executive team than they do about the business.

The idea that one area of the business is less important than another is dangerous. Organisations are like living organisms and, as such, meddling with one part will affect the others. If we really are to make lasting, serious changes within an organisation, we need a holistic view of the total business and how all the functions slot together to form the whole. To determine one small area of the business to be less important is like saying one part of the body is less vital than the rest — yet it is all parts, working in unison, which make us function healthily.

To continue this analogy, if we begin the infinite process of change in one small, so-called "non-vital" area of the business, it is like an organ transplant. When the surgeon first implants an organ, all our antibodies rise up to fight and reject this new part: they surround it, invade it, and do everything they can to have it removed. So it is with many of the businesses with which I have worked. Try to begin the process of change in one department and the other departments and managers attack these changes, aggressively or passive/aggressively, so rendering the change process impotent and thereby "proving" to those fighting against change that their original assertion was correct — "change does not work".

Whatever the motivation, the old Confucius wisdom seems to hold good:

> "Change is a door which can only be opened from the inside."

Creating a "Hawthorne Effect"

The Hawthorne studies of 1929 showed that it is relatively easy to produce short-term change benefits in an experimental situation. At the Western Electric Plant, Hawthorne, Illinois, two psychologists,

Roethlisberger and Mayo, increased the lighting in a particular section of the works and productivity in this area rose. Later, in the same section, they reduced the lighting, and productivity rose still further. This gave rise to the "Hawthorne Effect" — just by doing something, we get small change benefits.

Yet these changes soon disappear, along with the consultants who have worked for a short period with the company, achieved some "good" results, at face value, received the plaudits from "management" and moved on. Yet all that has happened is the delivery of a placebo and changes that do not endure, nor add any lasting value to the business. This is because real, lasting change takes time, courage, commitment and someone to make the management team look at themselves and, more importantly, start doing things differently.

It also requires the management team to be *prepared* to change, either from belief in the process, or from fear of failure or a desire not to be "left out".

Large-scale change can challenge deep-rooted values

I believe that the larger-scale the change process, the greater the likelihood of success. A large-scale approach goes fully across, and embraces, all areas of the business, redefining culture and values and bringing the dissenters out into the light where they cannot hide. This kind of change goes very much deeper than skill or technique; it goes right to the heart of who each manager is — not just what they do, but how they think, their intrinsic values and how they view the world and live their lives.

So when we tell managers that there is no easy solution, no pill to be swallowed, and that change must start with them as individuals, the message they receive is that they are failures, or that they are ugly/stupid/useless/unsuccessful. My point is that we often do not fully comprehend the extent to which such a message is taken, at an emotional level, as a personal attack. This can then manifest itself in the strangest of ways, but ways that can be tracked back to the original way the "message" was perceived and received.

Change sometimes involves letting go . . .

One CEO with whom I worked had been a brilliant entrepreneur and built up an expanding international business, which had begun in his garden shed. He was the perfect man for the job, curious, inventive, bright and, although a technical genius, not particularly people-oriented, or even business-oriented. He was the archetypal scientist — "I have invented something clever, someone must want to buy it!"

This, of course, carries with it even more difficult commercial responsibilities when the business is at "the leading edge" (often called "the bleeding edge"!). Such organisations are at "the mistakes end" of the market. They can see themselves as pioneers, forging new ground. But commercially, this means they are vulnerable; having climbed one peak, they are unsure if they have reached the summit or if there are other, possibly higher or more difficult, peaks to climb. Competitors wait in the wings, ready to learn from their mistakes and capitalise on them. So such organisations need a strong commercial hand.

In this case, once the organisation had reached £60 million, a hands-on technocrat (who would have secretly preferred to be on the benches) was not the right person to be CEO. And I had to tell him. For all his intelligence, he took this news badly, at an emotional level, and as a personal attack, citing all the things he had done for the business, rather than what was needed to be done in the future to grow an international company. He felt betrayed, let down, hurt and personally attacked, in what was a move motivated purely out of a desire to protect the business, his business. All the cash from a pay-off was little comfort to someone from an education system where failure was not to be tolerated. In his heart, he knew he was happier in a technical role and, to be honest, we are all either short or tall; it is not possible to be both. My advice to him was to go and do it all again. The creation, the start-up, is not only where his expertise lay, it is, more importantly, where all the fun, excitement and passion lie.

THE "BENCHMARKING" MYTH

Establishing world class standards or copying other people's tired, worn-out ideas?

You remember the old conundrum. A frog sits at the edge of a pond, 30 feet in diameter. He jumps exactly half way, and then half that distance, then half that distance, and so on. How long does it take him to cross the pond? The answer, as we all know, is "never".

I find continuous improvement a bit like this. As we seek constant incremental improvement, we may negate that single, creative, explosive quantum leap which freshens up the whole organisation or function and takes us a massive step forward. As organisations seek ever-evolving improvement, so the evolutionary process slows down, a bit like our frog on the pond. Often, a creative, revolutionary leap has to be built into the system or processes to prevent stasis, the stagnant pond of minuscule improvement.

The same problem can occur if we benchmark, especially if we benchmark too early. If Nissan, after the Second World War, had gone with their original intention of benchmarking against General Motors (the undisputed world leaders), their standards would have been considerably lower. Instead, they admired General Motors from a respectful distance, and decided to create their own standards.

So they got their creative heads together and said: *let's have a zero-based approach*. We know what we want to be. So, with no systems, standards, procedures, rules or benchmark to tie us down, how can we create a world class motor car manufacturer? Then, and only then, did they look at General Motors. The rest, as they say, is history. Nissan's meteoric rise to world prominence was almost as dramatic as General Motors' decline.

And the moral of this tale? Benchmarking, especially too early, may mean binding your organisation or function up with the tired old practices, ideas and standards of another organisation, and prevent you from realising your organisation's true potential. You may end up with Mediocre Inc!

The key is to establish our own values and to align our processes *and* behaviours behind this point. Measure ourselves against our values. How you measure the performance of your people will determine how they behave, which must be in a way that is absolutely consistent with our values. So, if our values really are values, then we will be happy to let our performance management, appraisal scheme — or however we measure performance — reflect this.

Then you can benchmark! You might well be surprised (shocked even), at how far ahead you are. A quantum leap, rather than slow, ponderous, incremental improvement will take our frog, not just to the other side of the stagnant pond, but beyond the pond, into fresher waters. The alternative is to dip your toes in the potentially stagnant water of "how others are doing things".

THE "EMPOWERMENT" MYTH

The Empty Car Park

The theory of "empowerment" is one against which it is difficult to argue, although the term has been overused and now sounds very 1980s. Yet in practice, it can lead to managers giving employees too much space too soon — like offering them an empty car park to park in. What happens when we drive into an empty car park? Given unlimited choice we often find the "choice" impossible and drive aimlessly around.

"Empowering" employees can also make managers feel "disempowered", and unclear as to how to fill their days or where they can now add value.

So many leaders attended the "empowerment" seminars in the 1980s and, totally impressed, having found "the way", came back and said to their staff, "You are empowered."

The staff took a look around, and nothing seemed different, and so they said: "What do you mean?"

"You are empowered!"

"What shall we do?"

"That's up to you now, because you are empowered!"

In their search for a panacea, many of these leaders failed to realise that, lofty aspiration as it is, *empowerment is a process*, not an event. We can't empower people; we can only begin a process which will begin to give those closest to the action the authority to make decisions, and to teach them how to make the best use of their decision-making power.

Is empowerment a "good thing" or a "bad thing"?

All the various schools of management over the past 20 years have preached the theory of empowerment. The notion is that we push decision-making as far down the line as possible to the people at the "sharp" end. Even mission statements allude to empowered employees.

I have met very few people who argue against the principles of empowerment, and I certainly would not myself. Yet the practical issues are perhaps not as clearly understood as the basic concept. Empowerment, in my experience, has a heavy downside — there, I've said it. The empowered 1980s were initiated in the context of the tight hierarchical structures that had typified industry. "Bosses", "secretaries", "typists" and "administrative staff" abounded.

In my first job in a shoe factory in Wellingborough, July 1971, aged 15, there was a clear distinction between "management", "staff" and workers" (three different toilets to begin with!) and, during the first few days, the supervisor explained that we were not paid to "think", but to "do". There was a factory manager, an assistant manager, and a supervisor over each section of about six people. We were told what to do and, conversely, this meant that unless we were told to do something, we didn't do it. Sometimes shoes would fall on the floor, or get damaged in some way and the supervisor would say, "pick that up", or "sort that out". It was only when we were told to do something that we did it. Pavlov's workers!

The supervisor would often come out to the toilet where someone would be talking about football, many would be silently smoking, someone else would be talking about their night on the town, another person would be making copious notes from *Das Kapital* for his Open University degree, and some may even be using the toilet for its original purpose. The supervisor would shout at us, "Get back to work!" To be honest, we sat and waited until he told us, and only then did we go back to work. If he didn't tell us to go back to work, then we wouldn't have known that we should, would we?

"Facilitative management" was seen to be the answer: to break structures and tradition and "empower" staff. However, this has caused a great many problems for some staff and managers. For many people, trust takes some time to build, and empowering staff requires a large investment of time and a huge measure of trust. During empowerment seminars in the 1980s, the "facilitator" asked, "Do you want to push decision-making as far down the line as possible?" "YES!" came the resounding reply. "Do you want to let staff take responsibility for their own destinies?" "YES!"

I wonder what sort of answer the facilitator would have got from questions such as, "Are you happy for your staff to make mistakes?" "Are you happy for your staff to take six times as long to come up with a decision than you would?" "Are you happy to invest time and money to create the processes to enable these great things to happen?" I wonder. It is all a question of how it is sold.

Freeing the slaves

Also, for staff used to a "command and control" system and mentality, to be suddenly told "You are free" can come as quite a shock. The "empty car park" syndrome, described earlier, meant many staff, used to working within the parameters of tightly structured job descriptions, had their safety nets taken away.

Job descriptions focused staff on filling their days with what the leader felt should be done (rather than what needed to be done) and ignoring how well it needed to be done. Suddenly, they were given more freedom than they were used to, or perhaps even wanted. Empowerment was supposed to be the vehicle through which staff were "allowed" to make mistakes, and the creation of a "no-blame" culture. I wonder whether it had that effect?

So one major problem with empowerment that we encounter frequently is leaders not giving enough time to effect the changeover of mindset necessary, nor understanding that, during this handover period, there need to be some signposts for staff to know they are going in the right direction. I have experienced leaders telling staff to take the initiative — another example of the paradox of management because, if you are telling someone to take the initiative, then *they* are not "taking the initiative".

Managers often say to me, as if they have been experimenting with a new type of Japanese lager, that they tried it and it didn't work, and so they go back to their original brand. They snap back to a command and control mentality, often with renewed vigour. No one has ever said leadership was easy; if it is an easy life you are after, don't become a leader.

Leaders' perceptions often mean they dip their toes in the waters of empowerment, rather than taking the leap of faith necessary, and, when it does not yield immediate results, they say things like, "He has a bad attitude, so it won't work." Whenever I hear a manager make such statements, what I hear is, "Bill, why am I such a poor manager of people that I can't get the best out of that person?" "Attitude", like "personality clash", is a convenient cop-out for not managing situations.

Also, empowerment has had the opposite effect and has led, in many cases, to leaders abdicating their responsibilities and retiring to their offices. One leader I spoke to from a building services company openly admitted he did not know, after initiating "empowerment" within his sphere of influence, how to fill his days meaningfully. And the notion of reading, and being seen to read, a pink paper, positively frightened him! There are times when a manager can feel "disempowered".

Perhaps one way of demonstrating power is to choose to give it up

Many leaders feel a loss of status and self-importance, which can cause great anxiety. This is, of course, no reason for not going through with it; it is just worth seeing the issue from the other side. Managers may feel a weakening of their power, yet, paradoxically, one of the best ways of demonstrating power is to give it up.

Perhaps the word "empowerment", which is sounding very jaded, dated and tired, should be replaced simply by "personal responsibility," with leaders supporting, challenging, cajoling, teaching and stretching their staff, to ensure responsibility is taken as well as given.

THE "COMMUNICATIONS SKILLS" MYTH

We often hear of leaders being sent on "communication skills" courses. Yet, once again, the key is that, if we want someone, or a group of people, to know something, then we will make sure they do. We don't need to attend a course for this, we need the desire.

Now I am not suggesting it is impossible to develop ourselves in public speaking, learning how to make more impactful statements, how to get a written point across in the best possible way. And yes, these belong in the box we call "communication".

In a large pharmaceutical company in the east of England, one of the senior managers was told he had to make some cost-saving cuts. Part of this package was to make his deputy redundant. Now, he was a "regular guy", the boss, a nice bloke, and had never been required to "do the deed" before. At the appointed hour, the deputy duly arrived, after much sweating and anguish on the part of the boss. He began with a long and convoluted speech about the "state of the nation", the need to change and how sorry he was that it had come to this. The deputy left, bemused and confused, a full hour later, feeling slightly sorry for his boss.

Unfortunately, due to the convoluted nature of the message, the deputy turned up for work the very next morning, totally unaware that he had been made redundant! The longer the message, the greater chance of confusion.

This guy could clearly have done with some help, some development in getting to the point, summarising what has been said, ensuring the other person has "got" the point. The problem, as I see it, is that many leaders hide behind the curtain of "communication skills" as a reason for not letting others know what is going on. "I haven't been on the course yet!"; "He lacks communication skills!" Maybe. But maybe he just won't make the effort to talk to his staff. Only once the effort has been made can we determine whether there are any gaps. I have had lots of experience, especially when going through a process of change, where leaders use "communication skills" as a blanket to hide under, and not get out there and tell people things they should, and want to, know.

THE "TIME MANAGEMENT" MYTH

It never ceases to amaze me how many "time management" programmes there are on offer. And I wonder if they create better leaders. How often do you hear, "I don't have time to attend a time management programme"?

I have seen the over-focus on the management of time negate all the small links and interactions with people that occur in a day, and keep the leader in touch. Chats by coffee machines, impromptu sessions with your team (or with other teams), all the seemingly inconsequential links and connections which form the rich pattern of a successful leader's life.

These courses teach us, "Close your door for four hours a day." I would answer, "And miss all the links with people which may never occur again?" I may also ask, "Why have a door?"

THE "APPRAISAL" MYTH

Someone once described the appraisal process as, "the annual reminder of who owns you"! This is often how it is. It's like sitting down with your spouse or partner twice a year to review your relationship. For the leader who is linked up to their staff, the "appraisal" is simply the formalisation of a process that is taking place day-by-day, week-by-week throughout the whole year. I'm certainly not knocking the principle of a formalised, recorded, two-way chat. But to make it "the event", rather than one event in a whole series of formalised and informal events, worries me. Nothing should come as a surprise at appraisal time.

THE "MISSION STATEMENT" MYTH

I worry about the amount of time, energy and effort that organisations expend in creating visions and mission statements. It's possible, in one trip, to visit a hospital to have a wound dressed, pick up a sandwich from the supermarket on the way back to work at the engineering company and see virtually the same mission statement in each venue. It's almost as though people feel that, where there is silence or white space, we must have words.

It is much the same with the declaration of values. One of our customers has, on the top line of a value statement, "We are committed to teamwork." Alongside this is a picture of a snowflake, looking lonely and fragile, and further down, a picture of a huge snowball bounding down a mountainside, with a statement along the lines of, "Look what happens when we stick together."

Yet when we look around the organisation, we find that no one sits in teams, there are no project teams and they pay individual bonuses. Surely if they were really committed to teamwork, then we would be able to find evidence, not just of teamwork, but of "anti-individualism"? Do they pay a team bonus? Do they sack individualists? Do they appraise staff in teams? Then don't say "committed to teamwork"!

Definitions are also important — using a common language that everyone understands. I was working with the main board of one of our customers to determine their "magnetic north". In trying to begin with some common ground, the Managing Director said, "Well, one thing we can all agree on is our desire for growth." They all nodded and suggested we move on from that point. I asked them what they meant by growth. They each looked at me with pained expressions and the Managing Director said, "I don't think we need to go into a Wittgenstein-type definition of the word growth." Yet when I asked each to define it, we had definitions ranging from "an increase in turnover", through "increase in customer base", to "higher profits"! Not only were these different definitions, they could actually be in conflict with each other. So sometimes asking the dumb questions like "What do we mean by . . .?" can be pretty smart.

THE "CORPORATE POLICY" MYTH

In this same organisation, the group Managing Director called me in to discuss one of his senior team. "It's Matt," he told me. "He's a great guy, has totally transformed customer service and the supply chain, and we desperately want to keep him and promote him."

"Great," I said, "what's the problem?"

"Well, I don't know how to put this, Bill. I see him going far in this organisation, he has the potential to go all the way. It's just that, well, I don't know how to say it . . ."

I was intrigued. Having recruited Matt and worked with him on several projects, I thought I knew him very well. I couldn't believe there could be such a serious problem. Maybe he had a medical condition? No, we checked this out when we recruited him. Maybe he had a personality disorder? No, we tested him. What on earth could be blocking such a talented guy from climbing the corporate ladder?

"It's, it's . . . well," Dan broke into a whisper, *"He's not a graduate!"*

I was incredulous. "Is that all?"

"You don't understand, Bill. In this corporation, you have to be a graduate to get above a certain level, that's company policy. So, what do we do, Bill?"

"You change your stupid policy!"

"No can do Bill, this comes all the way from the top." So we put together an elaborate plan to ensure that Matt got an MBA, thus qualifying him for a future within the corporation. Despite the fact that Matt was seen as the top-performing manager, that his appraisal and 360° assessment showed that he was streets ahead of his colleagues in so many areas, and that his people genuinely rated him as a manager. But being a non-graduate somehow made him less than human.

This is a perfect example of how policy-making among the top executives could have led to the loss of a real talent from the business.

THE "BETTER CONDITIONS CREATE A HAPPY WORKFORCE" MYTH

I once held to a premise, which I now believe to be a little shaky, that if we improve the lot of our workforce, it will automatically lead to a greater happiness factor. Experience has taught me a different story. History also tells us this is not so. Revolutions tend to happen after conditions have improved, once the process of change for the better is underway.

Remember the old men of China who, reluctantly, after years of autocracy, let go of the reigns slightly? In the ensuing years, they increased China's wealth and initiated many social reforms. Things weren't good, but they were better. Then we had Tiananmen Square . . .

People, previously unaware of their plight, suddenly realise, when given something extra, what it is that they don't have, and react accordingly. Historians call this "the theory of rising expectations". This is, in effect, the discrepancy between what people now have and what they believe it is possible to have. Psychotherapy is littered with such examples. As we resolve the primary issues, the issues affecting someone and which led to them seeking help, these lead to the secondary issues (often of a much higher order). So it does not lead to greater happiness or a sense of peace, but to going ever deeper to uncover ever-more painful issues. I guess if we open a can of worms, we must be prepared to see everything that is in there and deal with it.

Healthy and unhealthy "grumbles"

Abraham Maslow argues that the health of an organisation can be determined by the level of grumbles. In less healthy organisations, the grumbles are what he calls "the deficiency needs". For example, "The toilets are filthy"; "It's freezing in here"; "The pay is awful".

Yet strangely, in healthier organisations, the grumbles are of a much higher order, "I don't think my current role fully utilises my talents"; "We need a better health and safety policy to bring us up to European standards"; "I don't know why they just don't link the sales and marketing functions". The paradox is that it is only when organisations have raised standards and given workers a voice that we get the higher level grumbles.

So I say to leaders, don't expect improvement necessarily to bring about contentment; you might well find it does the opposite. This is not, of course, to argue against improving the lot of the workers — I would agree with that wholeheartedly. I just feel it is important to point out once again that there is no panacea and that management is a difficult game. As we will see below, with "positive stroking" not being the prime motivator many believe it to be, the principle of improvement is similar — making things better for people gives them a voice and raises their expectations. Do it, but don't think that it is the answer to your problems.

The ritualistic grumble of everyday communication

I also find, on my travels through organisations, that there is another type of grumble, what I call the "ritualistic grumble" of everyday communication. Two workers are talking and one says to the other, "How are you doing?" The other answers, "I would be much better if I didn't have to come to *this* place!"

Now, it would be easy to seize upon this conversation, see it as indicative of problems and take such statements as "proof" that morale is low among the workforce. However, such exchanges are often simply part of the general culture of the company, the way people talk to each other. If we explore the "real meaning" behind the statements, we find that there isn't one. It is simply the style through which workers communicate with each other, almost the way families have their own special language, phrases and sayings. Yet, I have seen many a consultant go into an organisation, interview the staff, and then get the management team together to explain how unhappy the people are, and how the organisation needs to change. All because of a few "ritualistic grumbles".

THE "POSITIVE STROKING" MYTH

Another example of this type of unexpected reaction is "positive stroking", or proactively praising employees. Once again, as with "empowerment", it is a difficult issue against which to argue, as, on the face of it, there can be no negative consequences. Yet, in my experience I have seen many instances of "overstroking" creating a halo effect around an employee, with negative consequence for that individual and others within the business. The management books say "positive stroking" is a great motivator, but I have seen many instances where it has the opposite effect, and where its value is less effective than other, more practical methods of motivation.

Excessive positive stroking can lead to unfulfilled dreams

One of our customers employed a bright young star whom the company had ear-marked for greater things. Although only 21, and with the company less than nine months, she had displayed a maturity beyond her years and had, according to the management team, all the ingredients they felt necessary for a higher position.

As such a position — key account manager for major multiples — was shortly to come up, the management team hinted, winked at and alluded to the fact that she would get the job. No promises, no formalising, nothing in writing. She didn't get the job.

When I spoke to her later, it provided an interesting learning point for me. I asked how she felt about being turned down. She explained that the hype had got to such a pitch that even her colleagues were telling her the job was in the bag, a forgone conclusion. So, at a psychological level, she imagined she had the job. The praise which continued to be heaped upon her led to her imagining she was already in the role, that she was successful in the role and, still further, she began to dream of the next role up the career ladder. At a more practical level, she began to live up to the £4,000 salary increase the new role would pay.

From management's point of view, they had done things by the book, given her lots of support and encouragement, and unfortunately she was simply pipped at the post by an external candidate. From the woman's point of view, she had been demoted and given a salary cut. All because of excessive positive stroking leading to unfulfilled dreams.

Saying "well done" to someone can bring the response, "how do you know?"

There are other reasons I have found why "positive stroking" may not be the great motivator we are often led to believe. It can be seen as a threat and, as such, received defensively. Praise is still an evaluation, a judgement of someone else and I have seen many people shy away from this. If you say to an employee, "well done", that person may well think, "I didn't know I was being watched." It can also be seen (and used) as a hierarchical stick with which to beat employees. The mere fact of giving praise is a clear signal that you are in the position to be able to give praise, therefore confirming and reinforcing the hierarchical authority. Also, we have to look to our own motivation in giving praise. Are we deliberately reinforcing our position of authority?

I remember one worker who used to squirm whenever her manager said, "Good morning to you."

Her rationale? "Who does he think he is that he can give me a good morning? Does he think he owns the morning?" Sure, a strange example, but people can smell insincerity a mile off and so we, as leaders, need to look to our own motivation. When we say, "Do you need any help?" we may be communicating, "I don't think that you are capable."

A spoonful of sugar may not necessarily help the medicine go down!

In the film *Mary Poppins*, Julie Andrews sang, "A spoonful of sugar helps the medicine go down". Some pseudo-enlightened managers have learned the (very) old adage: "praise and criticism in equal measure".

So, like Pavlov's dogs, staff *know* what is coming after a particularly heavy dose of praise. In this way, praise is used as a counter-balance to criticism, and so does not motivate the staff.

To give a converse example: I was working within a small engineering company in Cambridge where the engineering manager believed workers were paid only to work. Therefore the only time he spoke to any of the shop-floor staff was when he reprimanded them. As the door to the workshop was inordinately squeaky, every time he opened it the workers jumped, expecting someone to be told off and their behavioural reaction was to pretend to be busy.

The manager found it difficult to accept that he was in any way culpable (as managers often do!), yet he had to agree morale was low — and productivity even lower.

Praise and "positive stroking" may not, therefore, be the prime, easy motivators we have been taught to think they are. This is not to say that we should not praise or use "positive stroking" to good effect. People have come to expect it — we fish for compliments ourselves. Our education system awards gold stars for achievement — praise indeed. What I am saying is that people are more complex than we often imagine and quick-fix, buzzy solutions, easy as they appear, may not be what is required in a given situation and may not be the panacea we often believe.

Complex situations require more thought and need to be viewed from different angles and perspectives, according to the nature of the individual we are dealing with and the history and relationship we have with them. If we simply say, "Here is a sticky situation — a heap or two of praise will solve it", then we may be at best not understanding or helping the situation and, at worst, demonstrating abject laziness in our management approach.

THE "CHARISMATIC LEADER" MYTH

Even when I have met, and worked with, leaders who ooze charisma, who are lauded and praised, who seem to stand above all others, my dictum that there are no perfect leaders still holds true.

One of the most charismatic and inspirational leaders I ever worked with was the managing director of an engineering group. From the moment of his arrival, the organisation changed, morale lifted, and people began to behave differently. He set up project teams, got everyone talking, created a new customer-focused structure, brought manufacturing and sales together, and generally created the conditions where people wanted to be a part of the team. After a while, you could even recognise, at wider group meetings, those who were part of his team, Michael's boys. They stood out as more confident, better presenters and even charismatic themselves. They were all recognisable as "Michael's gang", the "A-team". They had a common language (including plenty of in-jokes), common dress and even a ritualistic bonding against common "enemies".

Michael put a lot of time into "his people", nurturing them, tasking them, drinking with them. His team worshipped him. When we ran a 360° assessment of Michael, his results were outstanding. Indeed, the only low scores were from Michael on himself! So, there we have it: a true success story, with no downside and no moral to the tale. Well, not quite!

You see, Michael was so charismatic that all those around him clung onto his shirttails. When we reflected on this, after he had made the decision to leave the organisation, there were some interesting issues. His charisma was such that everyone who worked for him raised their game.

But for many, this was a temporary state. Staff who were just regular people, or even those lacking talent, were suddenly bathed in the light of charisma. It was as if a whole raft of people, who previously had been unable to walk, suddenly began to stand up for themselves. However, as I pointed out to Michael, they were, in fact, clinging onto him, rather than standing up for themselves.

When he left the company, many of "Michael's gang" simply withered away. The light in which he bathed them was suddenly switched off and they went back to how they were before he arrived. All of Michael's charisma, positive attitude, drive and creativity, which he shared around, were gone. Because it all came from a single point: Michael!

So a major part of Michael's future development was to build processes and systems into his development of people, and to be able to give the bad news to staff, as well as the good. His people did not see their own weaknesses, as they were all part of the great and lauded team. Michael tried to protect them from unpleasantness and so they were never confronted by the mirror of reality.

Many have said of Michael that he needs no developing because he is the perfect leader. Even if we judge him as a leader on the performance of his people, we have to agree he was almost perfect. But when we judge him by the legacy he leaves within an organisation, then we can see that, as we all know, perfection does not exist. And we should *all* feel better for that fact!

THE "THAT'S HOW I AM AND I CAN'T CHANGE" MYTH

Many leaders adopt the view that "this is how I am and I can't change. People must take me as I am." Which is, of course, nonsense. View this person in a variety of situations: at work, at home with his or her children, watching a football match, at a job interview, down the pub with friends, etc. They display many facets of their character. This is behavioural modification according to the situation. So one major issue to get across is the difference between personality and behaviour.

Our personality is roughly set in the early years and remains reasonably constant throughout our lives. Personality is the result of the interaction between genetic conditions and environmental conditions in early life. It can therefore be represented in this way:

$P = (G \times E)$

Behaviour is the result of the interaction between personality and situation and so can be represented in this way:

$B = (P \times S)$

So changing circumstances and situations will lead to behavioural modification. Achieving behavioural modification is not the same as learning or acquiring new skills or knowledge; it is about situations making us alter the way we interact with other people. In fact, I would go further and say that much "skills" training, especially at management level, is actually a pretence.

It is also true to say that this formula explodes the old management myth of, "I can't change now; it is just my nature." For that we should read, "I choose not to modify my behaviour" — a slightly different angle. I have more sympathy for a leader who says, "I hear what you are saying, I understand the impact of my behaviour, but I don't care; I am taking a conscious decision not to change." I don't like the sentiment, but I admire the honesty.

THE "I NEVER GET PEOPLE WRONG" MYTH

In eighteenth-century England, those accused of stealing were often "branded" a thief. This word "branding" is not simply a metaphor in the way that we would now say someone has been branded a thief, but a literal branding to demonstrate to the world that this person cannot be trusted as they have been "proven" to have stolen from someone else. The branding, as well as being extremely painful, was designed to put an everlasting label on the "offender", so the world at large would know them for what they were.

We all still put such labels on people, though nowadays in the metaphoric sense! The old adage is, "When we first meet someone, we sum them up in 30 seconds." Yet that is only half the story, which actually should run, "When we meet someone, we sum them up in 30 seconds, and then we spend the rest of the time justifying our views." So, if we are interviewing someone and, in the first few seconds of the meeting we perceive them as being aggressive, we will, mainly subconsciously, phrase our questions in such a way as to ensure the other person gives aggressive responses, thereby "proving" our original assertion that they are aggressive. This behavioural modification is part of a theory called "transactional analysis".

Behaviour is interactive

This demonstrates both the interactive nature of behaviour and how the brain processes information. The brain seeks to build patterns and so follows a natural process to "prove" our assertions are correct.

The other person's behaviour will, to a large extent, be determined by our own behaviour, which is triggered by our perceptions and prejudices. This will, in turn, form the relationship. Our perceptions lead us to make judgements and making such judgements determines our behaviour. As behaviour is interactive, the other person's behaviour will be formed, in part, by how we behave. So many managers claim, "I know people." What they are actually doing is labelling people with their own perceptions and prejudices.

The perception loop

It was once assumed that the brain was like a hard disk drive, storing all our personal information (experiences, values, memories, etc.) in a grey box inside. We now understand that the brain is made up of billions of neurons, connected by a network of synapses, which carry electrical impulses. The way we access memory builds patterns into the neurons via the synapses, and this means that the more we think about something, the quicker the pattern is created. Preconceptions work *in exactly the same way* and form a "perception loop". This means that:

- How we view the world is formed by our experiences.

- These, in turn, form our perceptions (right or wrong!).

- These perceptions determine how we view other individuals.

- This will determine our own behaviour towards that person.

- Our behaviour towards them will determine how they behave towards us.

- This will "prove" to us that our perceptions were right all along.

- This will also reinforce our view of the world and the data we choose in making decisions.

Our preconceptions may be positive or negative, yet often they have the same impact. Managers often have a member of staff whom they believe is too "nice". By displaying this preconception, they may not stretch the individual, not push them into the firing line, not give them any projects which may be overly taxing, etc. By so doing, the person, like a flower starved of water, withers as an individual and this will "prove" the manager's original preconception about them being too "nice".

Everyone thinks they are fair

This is genuinely difficult for us to grasp, because we all, generally, believe we are fair and right in our views. How often do you meet someone to whom you take an instant dislike, yet after a period of time your views alter and you justify this by saying that the person has changed? Of course the person has not changed; it is our relationship which has changed, probably as a result of behavioural modification on both sides, and so a major shift in perceptions has taken place. Our brains actually seek out evidence that we are right in our assertions, thereby proving we "know" people.

This can also cause us to blame others for our own mistakes and shortcomings. Psychologists call this "transference of guilt". This is often unconscious in that we don't mean to blame others, but we look outside ourselves when things go wrong.

I remember the first time I went to dinner with my future wife's parents. My future mother-in-law was so nervous she was shaking as she served. She went into the kitchen to get the potatoes, carried them carefully in and, just as she reached the table, dropped the whole bowl on the floor. Immediately, she turned towards my wife and said, "Denise, now look what you've made me do!" It wasn't so much that she wanted to blame Denise, but wanted to be rid of the blame herself.

THE "GOOD AND BAD TRAITS" MYTH

It is so easy to see particular traits as "good" or "bad" when, in reality, they just are, and our own perceptions and prejudices decide if they are "good" or "bad". For example, if an individual is agreed, by two colleagues, to be detail-oriented, then their descriptions of him to other colleagues, based on their individual interpretations and prejudices, might be totally at odds with each other.

For example, the first colleague may describe him as, "staid, rutted, rule-bound, intransigent, unmoveable, can't be persuaded, slow, over-methodical, too detailed, inflexible . . ."

The other colleague may describe the same person, and the same character trait, as, "conscientious, good attention to detail, dots his i's and crosses his t's, doesn't get it wrong, careful . . ."

Both describe the same person and the same trait, but both accounts are strongly influenced by the perceptions each has of the particular person and his character. So which is right? *Neither, or both.*

One of our customers, a regional manager with a service organisation, is variously described as "cold and overbearing", and "caring". Now, the senior team simply put this down to the different ways his staff and colleagues relate to him or like his "style". Yet the reality is more complex. He is the archetypal patriarchal leadership figure. The "upside" of a father figure is the nurturing, protective character. However, the downside is a punitive, "I know best", controlling character. These are simply two sides of the same person.

He could not understand why, when he was such a caring leader, that his staff could possibly conceive of him as being anything other than cuddly, warm and protective. He did not see the downside of this characteristic. It is often worth exploring a characteristic and examining both sides before making value judgements about a person.

Dennis

We were asked by an engineering contract group to bring in a new head of contracts. They were a major supplier to a local food company, and needed a person to ensure they negotiated all contracts to their maximum benefit.

"Find us a real Rottweiler," the managing director told us. I asked why. "Nailing out contracts with favourable terms is the life blood of our business. We are getting screwed. We need a real animal."

So I found Dennis. Dennis was a real toughie, not a pretend one. He was cold, tough, non-relational and made decisions based only on empirical logic, never emotion. The company loved him. He was everything they dreamed of in a head of contracts.

I called them two months later to see how he was doing. They were over the moon with Dennis. He had re-negotiated some excellent contracts, and had tightened up the procedures and processes to ensure they negotiated from a much "harder" standpoint.

However, they did say something very interesting. "He's great at his job, Bill, and he's certainly made a real difference, but he's not exactly Mr Fun, and he never comes down the pub with us after work!" Isn't it interesting that they thought Dennis could switch off and put on a different head once work was over?

For Dennis, work was never over. And if you want a real hard, tough-minded, totally focused individual, there will be upsides and downsides to this trait. Character traits are not "good", or "bad", they just "are"!

THE "WHAT YOU SEE IS WHAT YOU GET" MYTH

Neil, the "supremely confident" manager

One of the brightest stars with whom I have worked was plucked from the obscurity of the internal sales/customer care function of a milk producer. I brought him in as customer service manager, and he rose to the dizzy heights of main board director within a major FMCG company and has since moved onto even greater things within a US engineering group. Neil is the archetypal working class boy who pulled himself up by his bootstraps.

He began life as a no-qualifications factory worker, and is now a senior executive. So he has completely changed, transformed even? Not quite!

Neil is described as supremely confident, fearless, hard-working and at the forefront of innovation. Everyone admires him. Yet when we strip away the veneer, we see the same under-confident, scared, working-class boy, afraid that he will be found out. Or worse still, that he will wake suddenly from an amazing dream, with his mum's voice and the alarm clock both ringing in his ears, telling him that it is 7.00 in the morning, and that he needs to get out of bed now or he will be late for work at the factory. Neil has told me so on many occasions.

F. Scott Fitzgerald's *The Great Gatsby* ends with the words:

> "Gatsby believed in the green light, the orgiastic future that year by year recedes before us. It eluded us then, but that's no matter — tomorrow we will run faster, stretch out our arms further . . . And one fine morning —
>
> So we beat on, boats against the current, borne back ceaselessly into the past."

In the same way, Neil's driven character is born out of an overwhelming desire not to go back. Paradoxically, when watching him in action, it is transparently clear that his confidence comes from having no confidence. His fragile nature is built on the rocky foundations of his past, and so this means he must always look forward (hence "supremely confident, hard working and at the forefront of innovation").

When Neil is described as one of life's success stories, a person who always strives to achieve, it is true.
It is also only part of the story. Neil is best at difficult
challenges. Give him a mountain to climb and he
won't look down, he will never look back. Yet this is
"because of" his lack of confidence, not "despite" it.
As Wordsworth wrote, "The child is the father of the
man." We cannot escape our pasts, but they can be
very useful in motivating us to achieve great things.
Motivation works in two ways: coming from and going to. In Neil's case, he clearly knows where he
doesn't want to be, and so this drives him relentlessly
forward.

The sad thing is that Neil has been so dynamic,
added so much value to the organisations where he
has worked, but he may never reflect on, or view, any
achievement as anything other than, "I got away with
it again, I have not been discovered." It means his
employers will get a good deal, and it means that Neil
will earn a lot of money and a lot more recognition.
But he has created for himself a hamster-wheel existence, a treadmill where he will be judged, not as a
person, but as a performer. Motivating Neil is no
problem; the hard part is to get him to extricate the
person from the performer.

He will continue to spin on, being known for what
he does, rather than for who he is: dynamic, talented,
but never allowing himself to reflect on a job well
done. Stopping for a minute might allow others to see
the real Neil. When leaders talk of motivation, what

gets people out of bed in the morning, the focus tends to be on what they are moving towards. As we can see with Neil, in examining motivation, it is always worth looking at the "coming from" as well as the "going to".

Tom, the teambuilder

Tom had one of the best reputations as a great leader of anyone I have known. When he left a heavy engineering company as sales director and took over as managing director of an electronics company, everyone assumed he would be a great success. His reputation as a decisive leader, a motivator of people and, most importantly of all, a builder of great teams went before him (and behind him). People used to sit around tables when times got tough and say, "If only Tom were here, he'd lead us out of this mess." He had attained an Eric Clapton-like aura around him.

When he and the electronics company parted, he asked me to conduct an objective assessment of his strengths and weaknesses in order that he get it right next time. After going through the full half-day battery of assessment systems, Tom, to my surprise, came out low on decisiveness.

Not only low, but extremely low. All the contra-indicators had him down as needing a lot of support in making up his mind. Once again we have a "despite versus because" situation. It was "because" of his inability to make decisions and need for input that he built great teams (and called me as well as other consultants in). This was why his teams were so good, and why they were encouraged to voice their opinions. Tom was a great empowerer of people — because he had to be! His words took on a new resonance after the testing process. When Tom says, "Bill, it would be great to bounce some ideas around", he means "I need some advice".

Both Tom and Neil are perfect examples of the complexity of leadership and how we often find that individuals display talent "despite", rather than "because of" their basic personality characteristics or backgrounds. People are far more difficult to understand and what we see isn't always what we get. But by thinking, and searching, a little more deeply, we can get to the "real" person. Not out of some morbid fascination or intellectual challenge, but because we need to understand the whole person if we are going to be able to lead them.

THE "MY BEHAVIOUR HAS NO BEARING ON OTHERS" MYTH

One of our customers called me for advice. "Why are all my staff such miserable whingers, Bill?" she whinged miserably at me. Now this may seem simplistic, but the fact is, just as parents are a major determining factor on the behaviour of their children, so leaders have a similar determining factor on the way the people they lead behave. Whenever leaders come to me and complain about the behaviour of the people they lead, and bemoan the fact that they cannot "find the answer", I hold up the metaphoric mirror to them and tell them to begin there. It is amazing how our own feelings are reflected in the actions of those we lead. We call this "modelling the way". When I explained this to the customer, she laughed and made the connection. Such simple connections are often overlooked in our desire to "do good".

She had, since being made Divisional Director, become totally hung up on budgets and profit. Now, businesses have to make a profit, and the development work we were undertaking with her had led to a greater focus on the numbers. However, this focus became an obsession, to the exclusion of everything else. And she did not realise the impact of this. I suggested she reflect, and in her reflection she came up with the idea that the numbers were low because her people were miserable and whingy, not realising this was simply a reflection of her own misery, her own behaviour towards staff.

In an advertising agency where we were asked to help them determine their "magnetic north", the future shape of the business, the Managing Director spoke to me about the values he wanted his business to reflect. "Fun, teamwork and target-driven", he enthused. Yet, he is a serious guy, shy, threat-sensitive and inhabiting the only closed office in the whole agency! There is often a large, but unaccepted, discrepancy between what a leader wants and what they are. So many leaders just do not recognise the impact they have on their business, and their people.

THE "HE'S TO BLAME" MYTH

One of the leaders I was tasked with helping develop had been through a "top drawer" education. BSc, MSc, two years at a college in France and more courses than a professional golfer. Yet he still did not understand the impact of his behaviour. Tony is a lovely guy, extremely bright and articulate, not prone to bouts of self-congratulation, but he simply smiled and rationalised any criticisms of his leadership or team behaviour. He could not see there was a problem. He, with 24 other leaders from all over the world, had been on an International Leadership Programme in Brussels. This Programme lasted 18 months, in ten two-week blocks. The "blocks" cover the so-called "hard" topics of Strategic Marketing, Finance, Ethics, Mergers and Acquisitions, etc. I teach what they term the "soft" subject of "understanding people"! I find it very strange, but it seems to me that the "soft" issues are always the hardest!

I was invited to spend four days watching the group's work during their final, project-based section, when they were particularly stressed (the projects were to be presented to the group CEO), and there was fractiousness within the teams. This seemed the best way of teaching psychology to them, when they were under great pressure and we would thus have excellent, concrete, current examples.

One of the major issues to emerge was that people found Tony overbearing, with a tendency not to listen. Over the 18 months, this had built to such a pitch that his sub-group did not want to work with him. A previous psychologist on the Programme had taught the Myers Briggs Type Indicator to the group in a bid to demonstrate a personality model with which all could identify and through which they could learn to accommodate each other, with all their little foibles.

Instead of remaining a participant, Tony decided his greater grasp of the subject would qualify him to teach the others in the group and so he "helped" them understand their "weaknesses". He saw the model as an intellectual exercise. So when it came to my session, I decided to allow Tony to stare into the abyss, and see if this would help him.

On the Saturday morning, I was supposed to teach "team dynamics". But instead of teaching, I asked the whole group for some examples of anti-group behaviour. One by one, each cited Tony as a disruptive influence. As the clamour for his head grew, the language became more spiked and real anger was being expressed. People were giving examples from the previous year. After half an hour (an excruciatingly long time), when I saw that Tony had really stared into the abyss, I taught for half an hour on the interactive nature of behaviour. Then I was able to get some examples and turned this around on the rest of the group. Why had they not explained to Tony that his behaviour was having a negative impact? Weren't they, by their silence or talking about the subject behind his back, reinforcing this behaviour? Therefore weren't they also culpable in the process? There were many red faces around the room. I gave them all 20 minutes, as a group behind closed doors, to help Tony develop in this area. And yes, he has modified his behaviour to a great extent; he actively seeks feedback and listens to the views of others. Whenever he backslides, he remembers the abyss.

It was essential to hit someone like Tony hard with the impact of his behaviour; a gentle approach would be rationalised and intellectualised away. Yet it was also important to see his behaviour in context. There are very few situations where one person is totally to blame. The others in the group also needed to understand this — and learn from it too. There are no experts in leadership. Remember, an expert is just someone who is on page four, whilst you are still struggling with page three.

THE "PERFECT ORGANISATION" MYTH

The "perfect organisation" is never the one we work for. It is always the one "over there". And so we head "over there", and find that the "perfect organisation" is actually not that one, but the one "over there". The moral is: there are no perfect organisations, just as there are no perfect leaders, or perfect people.

So many management books and learned studies speak of creating "the learning organisation". Now, this is laudable stuff, but the more pragmatic among us will recognise that in shooting for the moon, we may reach the top of the Empire State Building.

Within any organisation in which I have worked, you could say that there are, on average, around 15 per cent movers and shakers, who take the initiative and act as a positive influence, and 15 per cent negative cynics. The 70 per cent in the middle are the moveable feast who will go with the flow, and follow the group that is in the ascendancy.

We are often encouraged to focus our energies as leaders on the 15 per cent cynics, in the hope that we can turn them around. But cynics are strange people. If we bash a cynic, we only make them more cynical, and if we take the positive route ("hey, I used to be like you") it can be an uphill struggle. Now I am not against transforming negative people *per se*. Indeed, in many of the organisations I have worked with, it has been a joy to take the more negative, even destructive people (recognising that they are bright but with very little outlet for their brightness other than mischief) and channelled these attributes in a more positive way, often into senior positions.

The problem I have is when leaders begin with the cynics, in a pseudo-philanthropic drive to "convert the wicked". This can cause the other 85 per cent to feel neglected, unloved, undervalued. Also, as the positive 15 per cent tend to be the ones with get up and go, they often get up and go! What are you then left with?

Structures and Strictures

I don't like organisation charts (organigrams). Not because it is hip and trendy to knock them, but because it forces people into boxes. One of the arguments against job descriptions is that they become demarcation lines, focusing individuals on doing "just the job and no more". They can lead to an inflexible workforce. I feel much the same about organigrams.

More and more, we need leaders who will get out of their boxes and start to walk a bit. And then a little bit further. PowerPoint is used so frequently now that, when deciding upon the shape of their organisation, we find leaders reaching immediately for the laptop, like some kind of magic box.

Even the teaching of strategy often still involves the MOST principle (Mission, Objectives, Strategy, Tactics). Yet this is an age where we talk constantly of flexibility and change.

We were asked by a top advertising agency to look at their structure with a view to a forthcoming merger. Now, these are intrinsically creative individuals, people who berate their clients for not constantly coming up with new ideas, innovations and ways of selling product.

Yet when we started looking at their own business, each reached immediately for their laptops and started drawing boxes with names in them. They moved from creative-radical to boring-conservative in an instant. Part of the reason for this is the word "structure", itself conjuring up an image of stasis and straight lines. Another is, of course, the nature of our society, which is still hierarchical and driven by titles. When I go to a party, someone invariably asks me, "What do you do?" They really don't want to know that I eat curries, drink lager, watch football, read lots, and ruminate on people mostly. What they mean is, "How do you earn your living?" (Incidentally, I try to avoid ever telling anyone I am a psychologist; otherwise they tell me, "You'd be interested in me!")

THE VISION FOR THE FUTURE

In deciding the most appropriate shape for your business, or department, or function, it is good to determine your "magnetic north". "Where are we going with this company?" Just as history was passed down by word-of-mouth, often using strong imagery, colourful language, and story format, so too should your vision for the organisation or function be communicated. Your vision for the future needs to be compelling, interesting, understandable, believable and motivating. It needs to create meaning in peoples' lives and in their contribution to the organisation. It needs to animate people by bringing to life your vision of what the organisation will look like. I have sat in on too many presentations where the CEO has bored the audience into submission, whilst trying to explain where the business is going. People generally do not think numerically, and too much hard data does not aid digestion.

I sat in on a presentation from the CEO of a Swedish engineering group at a conference centre in Hertfordshire. He spoke for over two hours, and the first "light" went out after only seven minutes. He asked me for some feedback on his performance, and then complained, "But I gave them all the information."

In trying to provide as much detail as possible, the CEO switched off his audience, none of whom could remember anything of the presentation. He created a maze, an assault course for the brain. The key is to make it interesting, relevant and short. If a CEO can't articulate the vision so that everyone understands it in 20 minutes, the audience will be left cold.

This also illustrates another problem: senior executives saying, "How was I? Tell it to me straight." What they are really saying is, "Lie to me and tell me I was wonderful." When people say they can take criticism as long as it's constructive, I tend not to believe them! I have not met many people who genuinely take criticism well without intellectualisation, rationalisation or temper tantrums.

So you need to organise (not structure) your processes and behaviours behind the "magnetic north". If we really live in a world of perpetual change, then we must keep any structures light, nimble, flexible and ready to move as the world turns. Sure, organisations (especially larger organisations) need some structures. However, the future holds lots of surprises and the better organisations are the ones that are flexible enough to be able to change when necessary.

THE ROLE OF "THE LEADER": A FINGER ON THE PULSE, OR AT THE BEATING HEART OF THE BUSINESS?

We have all experienced the majority of the "myths" outlined in this chapter. I said at the beginning of the book that it was about you. And I meant it. Leadership is not an intellectual exercise or a difficult science or a mathematical formula. Less still is it a gatepost through which only the "trained" can pass! It is all about you: making the best of what you have and so becoming the leader you are capable of being. Yes, you will backslide; yes, you will make mistakes. But if you are building the team around you, behaving with integrity, getting in close with people, then you will be forgiven. The key is to bring out and develop the leader in you, to keep focused, keep watching, keep learning. And when you think you have it taped, that is when you really need to start taking serious stock!

Dressing Up

Dale Carnegie once said, "If you want to be a Managing Director, start dressing like one." The less discerning took this advice at face value and bought posh suits. However, I think such individuals are missing the point. I think this quote refers to behaviour, not dress. Maybe a less subtle paraphrase of the quote might be, "If you want to be a Managing Director, start acting up." Not dressing up, or sucking up, but acting up. Start *behaving* like a Managing Director!

Now one of the problems with this (although I don't disagree with the sentiment) is that many have seen this as a way of developing "the technique" — "dressing" like their favourite leader (be it John Harvey Jones, Richard Branson or Anita Roddick).

The better leaders, in their own way, bring out their own best, transcending mere fads and "techniques"; they bring out the unique leader in themselves. This is not some kind of "new age" idea about "finding ourselves" or self-actualisation. This is at the heart of what this book is about, part of the title. It is about becoming your kind of leader, realising your potential, making you better at what you do, rather than trying to be like your hero.

Most of the leaders I work with need, and want, more than a finger on the pulse of the business. They need to be an integral part of the whole beating heart of the company. In fact, one of the muscles making it beat. Facilitative management can be remote control management, too "hands off", and managers, more than anything else, must be connected. Leaders need to lead, to be busy, to act as the "glue" to ensure that all the component parts are connected. Yet the "myths" pervade.

I took a group of managers from a large food organisation to help them determine their "magnetic north". Knowing the team reasonably well, I had a concern over their energy levels. So as part of the process, at 8.00 p.m. on the evening of the first day, after a real slog, I handed each a paper containing a synopsis of the major themes of a particular philosopher; one had Wittgenstein, one Descartes, etc. The Supply Chain Manager complained to me about this. "I have asked for three years to attend a 'presentation skills' course, and it hasn't happened," she said. "How can you expect me to participate in this if I haven't been on the course?" Yet she is the same person who fought bravely for her corner during the "magnetic north" session, who was very articulate in putting her arguments forward on how the supply chain needed to change, etc. She is bright, has opinions and voices them. But if you *ask* her to present,

she remembers, somewhere deep in her unconscious, the myth that "only those who have been on
the magical course, who have been trained, can present their ideas". Despite this, she may have spent
several hours "presenting" them (in a very persuasive manner!) at the bar the previous night!

The point is, it was not about presentation "skills",
but about confidence, and about the fact that, although she actually was a persuasive speaker, she
saw the exercise as a "presentation" and so reached
straight for the "training vocabulary" and said, "I haven't been on the course." In discussions afterwards,
she realised that what I was doing had nothing to do
with presentation or skills but about having the ability
to assimilate unfamiliar information and share it in an
interesting way.

It is all part of the myth, that managers are created,
like Frankenstein's monster, on training courses. Or
that "positive stroking" or creating better conditions
will make everyone happy. Or that going on a time
management course will magically transform your
day. Or that burglars always wear striped jerseys and
black masks! At best naïve; at worst a copout.

Break free from the myths. What organisations
need now, more than ever before, in these turbulent,
exciting times, are leaders who will "step out of the
boat", who will genuinely lead people and who will
take the time, trouble and effort to get to know their
"raw materials" — the people they lead.

———✡———

Part 2

360° Assessment

Before you can become a great leader of people, you must know people. Before you can know other people, you must know yourself. The first step in leadership — and possibly the hardest — is therefore to "look in the mirror", examine your own behaviour and its impact, determine the areas that need improvement and development, and then do something about it.

"Looking in the Mirror": The Concept of 360° Feedback

"O wad some power the gift tae gie us, to see ourselves as others see us." — *Robert Burns*

Imagine someone shows you a piece from a photograph — just one small corner — and asks you to interpret and comment on the whole picture. It is simply not possible to make a balanced judgement. Yet that is often what we are expected to do when we appraise staff, or make career, development and performance judgements, based on the one-dimensional information generated from our own perceptions.

The 360° feedback process is like holding a mirror up to ourselves, allowing us to "see ourselves as others see us". This means seeing the full picture, by gaining inputs from a variety of sources — boss, colleagues, direct reports, customers, even friends and family, in order to provide a more objective and balanced view of the impact of our behaviour. We may not like "looking in the mirror", but this is our starting point for self-development.

Personality and Behaviour

Remember our earlier discussion about the difference between personality and behaviour? To recap: personality is the result of the interaction between "Genetic Conditions" and "Environmental Conditions" (P = G x E). *Therefore, personality, once set, does not change.* Behaviour, on the other hand, results from the interaction between "Personality" and "Situation" (B = P x S). *Therefore, behaviour can be modified if we choose.*

This negates the argument that there are "personality clashes", or managers who say, "that's how I am", or "people can take or leave me". It can also help to combat the old chestnut of "attitude problems". Whenever I hear that expression it makes me shudder. "Attitude problem", like "personality clash", is a convenient box into which people or situations can be placed rather than dealt with and managed.

I was called by the distribution manager of a large company about the performance of one of his staff. "Bill, I wonder if you can help me; one of my staff has an attitude problem."

I was puzzled. "An attitude problem?" I asked.

"Yes, a problem with his attitude."

"What exactly is that?" I asked.

"I thought you were the psychologist," he replied angrily!

When I began to explore with him what the issues really were, we had to almost go back to basics:

"What is he currently doing that you would like him to stop?" "What is he currently not doing that you would like him to start?" Once again, the key is to get to basic behaviours, and the impact of these. Silly expressions like "attitude problems", or "personality clash" obscure some fundamental issues. People, and situations, have to be managed. Whenever I hear of a "personality clash", I think that there are two individuals unwilling to modify their behaviours to accommodate the others, or a manager looking for an easy term to explain away the situation, rather than deal with it.

We can all modify our behaviour, and this is the best basis for continuous development. Behaviour is choice, and the acceptance of this concept carries with it a certain responsibility. So, once we have "looked in the mirror", we have a decision to make: "Am I prepared to do something about it?"

It may be that we don't like what we see, it may be that we find it difficult to accept. It may even be that we are surprised how good our reflection looks! The key is that, whatever the picture, we cannot escape a process which measures the impact of our behaviour on other people and so captures their experiences. This reflection is too important to ignore.

Not for the faint-hearted . . .

The questionnaire that follows is designed to help you take the first steps towards understanding the impact of your behaviour. There are no right or wrong answers. Maybe you'll want just you and one other colleague whom you trust to complete the questionnaire, to begin the process of gaining a balanced perspective. So often, when leaders undertake 360° assessment, they are surprised at the results, even though it is those around whom they work, day-by-day, who complete the questionnaires. So don't be overly critical of yourself or anyone else! This is an excellent opportunity for YOU to find out how you come across and then plan to do something about it.

We all kid ourselves; we all look in the mirror and see the person we want to see, rather than necessarily the person we really are. Deep down, we know what we are like, but often don't want to look, and so we subconsciously see ourselves in the best possible light. But the key with 360° assessment is that we learn the *impact* of our behaviour.

So go on, look in the mirror! I remember once when my dad shaved off a huge drooping moustache, he complained that he looked much older — not realising he *was* much older, having had the moustache for ten years! Yes it may be a shock, yes it may be painful, but this will be a measure of how serious you are about developing. It means moving out of your comfort zone; it means facing up to painful truths; it may even mean a realisation that you are not the leader you once thought. However, we can all look like Arnold Schwarzenegger. It is simply a question of what we are prepared to give up for it. Now there is your acid test!

The 50-item questionnaire should be completed by you and up to five others who know you well and upon whom your behaviour impacts on a regular basis. The first step will be photocopying or reproducing the questionnaire, and actually giving it to people. Try to get completed questionnaires from colleagues, direct reports and your boss so that you have a reasonable balance of scores. Maybe even, if it is possible, get those outside the business (customers, suppliers, family, friends, ex-colleagues, etc.) to complete a questionnaire on you. The biggest issue is to get the fullest possible picture of how your behaviour impacts other people. Only this perspective will provide the foundation for development.

SELF-ASSESSMENT QUESTIONNAIRE

	Always	Most of the Time	Some of the Time	Rarely	Never
1 Sets high standards for all staff	5	4	3	2	1
2 Acts as a coach and a mentor	5	4	3	2	1
3 Is seen as a role model	5	4	3	2	1
4 Acts as a role model	5	4	3	2	1
5 Staff are consistently learning and developing	5	4	3	2	1
6 Continuously seeks feedback on impact of leadership style	5	4	3	2	1
7 Modifies behaviour in the light of feedback	5	4	3	2	1
8 Is aware of the impact of own behaviour	5	4	3	2	1
9 Learns from mistakes and failures	5	4	3	2	1
10 Understands own strengths and weaknesses	5	4	3	2	1

	Always	Most of the Time	Some of the Time	Rarely	Never
11 Utilises the strengths of the whole team	5	4	3	2	1
12 Really cares what people think	5	4	3	2	1
13 Is clear when to provide support	5	4	3	2	1
14 Is clear when to let people get on with it	5	4	3	2	1
15 Demonstrates an interest in others	5	4	3	2	1
16 Demonstrates high personal standards	5	4	3	2	1
17 Takes responsibility for own mistakes	5	4	3	2	1
18 Faces up to difficult situations	5	4	3	2	1
19 Is fair	5	4	3	2	1
20 Is trusted	5	4	3	2	1
21 Treats everyone as an individual	5	4	3	2	1
22 Is consistent in words and actions	5	4	3	2	1
23 Creates a no-blame culture	5	4	3	2	1
24 Encourages open working relationships	5	4	3	2	1
25 Welcomes ideas from all sources	5	4	3	2	1

	Always	Most of the Time	Some of the Time	Rarely	Never
26 Adapts well to changing situations	5	4	3	2	1
27 Encourages new ideas and initiatives from staff	5	4	3	2	1
28 Challenges the status quo	5	4	3	2	1
29 Moves with the times	5	4	3	2	1
30 Seeks better ways of doing things	5	4	3	2	1
31 Sees the "bigger picture"	5	4	3	2	1
32 Links functional issues to the grand plan	5	4	3	2	1
33 Is future-oriented	5	4	3	2	1
34 Creates a sense of ownership of functional goals	5	4	3	2	1
35 Develops nimble and flexible structures	5	4	3	2	1
36 Argues logically and persuasively	5	4	3	2	1
37 Is listened to	5	4	3	2	1
38 Wins others around	5	4	3	2	1
39 Negotiates well at all levels	5	4	3	2	1
40 Is respected	5	4	3	2	1

	Always	Most of the Time	Some of the Time	Rarely	Never
41 Completes tasks	5	4	3	2	1
42 Plans to have no surprises	5	4	3	2	1
43 Develops contingency plans	5	4	3	2	1
44 Co-ordinates work flow	5	4	3	2	1
45 Sets out clear responsibilities	5	4	3	2	1

	Always	Most of the Time	Some of the Time	Rarely	Never
46 Keeps people informed	5	4	3	2	1
47 Is direct	5	4	3	2	1
48 Keeps it jargon-free	5	4	3	2	1
49 Is listened to	5	4	3	2	1
50 Speaks well in groups	5	4	3	2	1

Collate the results . . .

Use the Results template to collect and correlate the scores from the questionnaires returned to you.

In the "Self" column, write in all of your scores in descending order. Do the same with questionnaires from colleagues, customers, friends, etc. (A, B, C, D in the template).

Calculate your "average" score in each perform-ance area by adding all scores in that column, and dividing the total by 5. Put the average score in the relevant column and do the same with each question-naire received back.

To calculate the "Overall average", add up all of the "average" scores and divide this total by the number of questionnaires returned (including your own).

SELF-ASSESSMENT RESULTS

The Leader as Teacher	Self	A	B	C	D
1 Sets high standards for all staff					
2 Acts as a coach and a mentor					
3 Is seen as a role model					
4 Acts as a role model					
5 Staff are consistently learning and developing					
Average					
Overall Average					

Understanding of Self	Self	A	B	C	D
6 Continuously seeks feedback on impact of leadership style					
7 Modifies behaviour in the light of feedback					
8 Is aware of the impact of own behaviour					
9 Learns from mistakes and failures					
10 Understands own strengths and weaknesses					
Average					
Overall Average					

Awareness of Others	Self	A	B	C	D
11 Utilises the strengths of the whole team					
12 Really cares what people think					
13 Is clear when to provide support					
14 Is clear when to let people get on with it					
15 Demonstrates an interest in others					
Average					
Overall Average					

Values	Self	A	B	C	D
16 Demonstrates high personal standards					
17 Takes responsibility for own mistakes					
18 Faces up to difficult situations					
19 Is fair					
20 Is trusted					
Average					
Overall Average					

Managing Diversity	Self	A	B	C	D
21 Treats everyone as an individual					
22 Is consistent in words and actions					
23 Creates a no-blame culture					
24 Encourages open working relationships					
25 Welcomes ideas from all sources					
Average					
Overall Average					

Change Tolerance	Self	A	B	C	D
26 Adapts well to changing situations					
27 Encourages new ideas and initiatives from staff					
28 Challenges the status quo					
29 Moves with the times					
30 Seeks better ways of doing things					
Average					
Overall Average					

Leader as Designer	Self	A	B	C	D
31 Sees the "bigger picture"					
32 Links functional issues to the grand plan					
33 Is future-oriented					
34 Creates a sense of ownership of functional goals					
35 Develops nimble and flexible structures					
Average					
Overall Average					

Influence	Self	A	B	C	D
36 Argues logically and persuasively					
37 Is listened to					
38 Wins others around					
39 Negotiates well at all levels					
40 Is respected					
Average					
Overall Average					

Management of Systems	Self	A	B	C	D
41 Completes tasks					
42 Plans to have no surprises					
43 Develops contingency plans					
44 Co-ordinates work flow					
45 Sets out clear responsibilities					
Average					
Overall Average					

Management of Information	Self	A	B	C	D
46 Keeps people informed					
47 Is direct					
48 Keeps it jargon-free					
49 Is listened to					
50 Speaks well in groups					
Average					
Overall Average					

Once you have the completed results, transfer all total scores into the Leadership Profile. Thus you will have a clear picture, driven numerically, of how you are currently performing as a leader, as perceived both by you and by those around you.

LEADERSHIP PROFILE

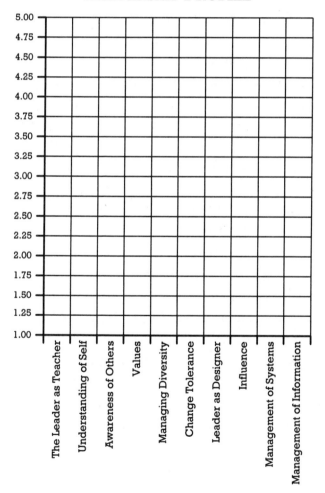

The key is not to get hung up on each individual score, although it usually makes very interesting bedtime reading (we are all our own favourite anecdote!). Try to look at the overall pattern and take the lowest areas as the focus for your development. If there is an imbalance, it simply demonstrates that different people see you in different ways, but their perception is their reality, so don't ignore the reflection in the mirror. One leader we assessed, the managing director of a chemical plant, was pleased with his results, which showed consistently high scores. "What do you think of these, Bill?" he asked. "That your people have very low standards!" I replied.

Seeing this in black and white can be quite traumatic, but it helps to see it as the starting point, a snapshot in time, rather than a profile for life. There is an excellent trade-off here. If we accept the profile as a behavioural-based assessment formed from the experiences and perceptions of those around us, then we are much more likely to accept that we can modify our behaviour as a result of the information.

So, if there are some highs, this does not mean you should not bother about those performance areas. However, your first focus should be the three or four lowest areas. These are the areas where you will get your early "wins" and have the biggest impact. Remember, self-development is a journey, not a destination. It is also good to thank those who completed questionnaires on you and, if you are really brave, share your results with them and tell them the areas where you intend to focus your development.

If you want to lose weight, tell everyone they should expect to see major differences in you within three months! Development is the same. You will put yourself under healthy pressure by telling staff what they can expect to see changed about you in the coming months.

At one of our customer firms, we published the main areas for development of each member of the senior team in the staff canteen so that all staff were fully aware of where each leader, and the team as a whole, were going with their development. This certainly helped each leader focus their mind! It also ensured that staff saw specific behaviours which the team said would change, so it focused on outputs (i.e. what would be different), rather than inputs (i.e. what "courses" they would be attending).

The Dangers of Rationalisation

John, an ex-surveyor in the private sector, had a strong background in controlling subcontract labour on-site. Ten years ago, he became Amenities Head of Service for a local authority. He is tough, uncompromising, loves an argument, and his people are afraid of him. He laughs this off, puts it down to his gruff Scottish manner, and the fact that he likes to "tell it like it is". His people live in fear of him, have no respect for him and tend to keep their heads down and get on with the job in hand.

As part of their drive to become more "customer focused", the authority decided to re-appraise its vision and values, and develop more "people-driven" values. This would, of course, impact on the behaviours of the leaders and so the process was launched with a 360° assessment and feedback process for the senior team, of which John is a part. His profile was very bad, showing him to be a bully, task-focused and with little sensitivity or care for the people he leads. During the feedback process, John used excuses, explaining that people in the south were more prone to being over-sensitive, and found "logical" reasons for all his low scores. Although the process was totally confidential, he put pressure on staff to find the seven respondents who completed on him. His argument was that it would be more helpful to "have it out" with each of them "face-to-face". But those completing questionnaires on John were only so honest because they were guaranteed anonymity.

This is a perfect example of a leader having the mirror of reality held up to him, and rationalising, intellectualising and making excuses, rather than seeing the process as an opportunity to change and maybe begin to get his people "on-side". Just as, in business, customer complaints are a perfect opportunity to begin the process of change, and allow a re-appraisal of relationships, this was John's chance to do the same — and he blew it.

So part of the "self-discovery" process must be a willingness to face up to the perceptions of others, however painful. Their perceptions are their realities and it is a perfect opportunity to develop, learn about the impact of our behaviour and even turn back the clock on difficult or broken relationships.

In Part Three, the various "links" will help you raise your scores next time, and, more importantly, begin to improve your performance as a leader.

Talk to People outside of Work

If the "self-learning process" is a bit new and causes you concern, start with talking to people outside work who know you well. Ask for some honest (and gentle) feedback on you, a summation of how you are and how you come across. This will help you identify the areas where you need to behave differently. Remember, this is not designed to take away who you are as an individual, but can help you modify your behaviour so that you become a better leader of people.

Negative feedback can often evoke an automatic defensive response in us. We assume (even subconsciously) that we are being attacked and so it is natural for us to defend ourselves, isn't it? Yet, paradoxically, this defensiveness prevents other people from giving us the level of honesty we need to develop. Fighting against this tendency may be unnatural, but it will ensure other people give us the true picture, however painful this may be.

Part 3

Leadership's Missing Links

If the myths in the first part of this book represent the old, outmoded way of thinking on leadership, the "missing links" given here show the way forward. They are not links in a chain, however — binding "rules and regulations" like a "leadership procedure" that should be adhered to at all costs, lest you slip off the path of great leadership, even if there are many who would want such a blueprint. Rather, they are the connections forged in experience, the vital bonds that all great leaders, consciously or unconsciously, create around them. Many of them are common sense, but it is often common sense that gets left behind in the rush to develop leadership skills through training programmes.

FORGING LINKS

Forging links means building relationships and developing a complete understanding of the business we are in, including the people who make it all happen. In the old days of the 1970s and 1980s, "relationships" may well have meant long lunches, taking people out to wine and dine them. Now, very few people have time to do this. The modern definition of relationship is a common, fruitful, mutual understanding. When these links are "missing", they prevent us being the leader we are each capable of becoming through bringing out what is already in there.

The ideas that follow are designed to make you think about yourself: how you might be more fulfilled and add more value (and feel you are adding value) to your people, your department, your business, your customers and yourself. The better leaders I have worked with are those who are well connected. Not through any old school-tie connection, but through linking up with all the various people and issues that affect the business or function they lead. Being connected, "linked up", keeps us in touch, and when we are in touch we are more likely to be able to make the right decisions. I would not advocate being linked up for some philanthropic reason, but because of commercial reality. Businesses are complex, living organisms.

Only by breaking out of our own mindsets, climbing out of our boxes on the organigram, breaking down the four walls of our function or business and seeing everything as having an upstream and downstream, will we really have a true perspective on our business, on our people, on ourselves.

In *The Fifth Discipline*, Peter Senge uses an old tale by Sufi to illustrate the importance of "whole" thinking, of stepping outside your function in the organisation in order to see more clearly. In the tale, three blind men try to describe an elephant by touch, but as one is touching an ear, another the trunk and the third is touching a leg, their interpretations are very different. None of the three "sees" the whole elephant.

This part of the book will help you focus on the areas where you can become better connected and provides an array of ideas about how you might achieve this. Being connected is much more than just being in touch. It is about understanding the environment around which you work and which will have a major impact on your performance as a leader of people.

Leadership versus Management

What is the difference between "management" and "leadership", "managers" and "leaders"? When do you manage, when do you lead? Throughout this book, the main focus has been on the term "leadership". Determining your own definitions will help. If you asked me to define the difference between "management" and "leadership", it would in many respects be like the difference between "efficiency" and "effectiveness". "Efficiency" is doing things right, and "effectiveness" is doing the right thing. "Management" is about stasis and control, "leadership" is about movement and change. Both are at times necessary, but it is helpful to know when to manage and when to lead.

As leaders we need to be acutely aware of when to follow and when to lead; we need to recognise the difference in various situations. Knowing when to take charge is possibly the easier bit, and the attribute that is seen as most characteristic of sound leadership. However, in some situations, we must also be able to take advice and go with the direction of someone more senior or who is politically more "important". Learning when to lead and when to follow is essential for managers within all organisations. This is all part of being politically aware.

In getting managers to think about the leadership role in *The Fifth Discipline*, Peter Senge urges us to consider who is the "leader" on board a ship. While we would normally think immediately of the captain or the navigator, Senge argues that a much neglected leadership role is that of designer. Like a ship, an organisation that is poorly designed will sink, no matter how inspirational its captain is.

LINK TO YOURSELF

If we are to understand, manage and motivate others, we first need to recognise, study and be aware of our own capabilities, limitations and motivations. We need to know ourselves, what drives us and makes us tick. At appraisal time — in fact all the time — we should ask those on whom our behaviour impacts on a day-by-day, week-by-week basis what we should be doing differently, and why. Use 360° feedback (see Part Two), engage those you trust, get honest and painful feedback on you as a leader. The first principle needs to be "What am I like?"

Values and Diversity

How we view the world will have a major determining factor on how we perform as leaders. Most of us assume that we have no prejudices and that our values are simply "the norm". It is worth taking the opportunity to explore our own values, and how the values of other people may be very different. This does not make them wrong; simply different.

Understanding our own values is a great jumping-off point for understanding others, and this will help us bring out the best in them, which is, after all, the reason we get paid as leaders.

We also need to be clear in our own minds as to how what we do supports the organisational goals, know where we add value, and know where we are not adding value. Not how much time do we spend at work, or even how much do we care, but where are the areas we add real value and make a difference? Write in one paragraph your own mission statement for your role, beginning, "The key focus for this role is to . . . " Then you will have absolute clarity as to why your job exists and the unique contribution it makes to the function, the people, the organisation. If you cannot adequately define, in a sentence, why your job exists, then maybe it shouldn't.

LINK TO OTHER MANAGERS

We all need to learn to understand people. We should actively analyse others, suspend judgement, try harder, focus on known behaviours and not perception, and learn what makes others tick. A good starting point is the acceptance that we are all motivated by different things. The next is to get other peoples' perspectives. Valuing diversity will also help prevent cloning, i.e. recruiting and promoting in our image.

Find out the challenges facing other managers, the successes, opportunities, the frustrations, in order to get hold of the bigger picture. This can only be accomplished by moving out of your own function and getting closer to managers in other departments. Only then will you have a true, broad perspective of your organisation.

LINK TO YOUR BOSS

The concept of "managing upwards" is often a neglected one in leadership development. Yet it is such a crucial issue. Rather than complain about how we are "treated" by the person who manages us, 50 per cent of the responsibility for managing this relationship is ours! Scary thought, isn't it? We need to question, "Am I a passive recipient of the actions of my boss?" Managing upwards is the art of consciously and proactively improving the relationship with your boss to achieve the best personal and organisational outcomes. The key questions are:

♦ What does your boss want from you? What does he or she want to hear and need to know?

♦ What do you want from your boss?

♦ What are your boss's priorities?

♦ Are your own goals and priorities compatible with those of your boss?

The key is to initiate regular, one-to-one meetings with specific agendas. Such meetings have a positive effect on team effectiveness *and* productivity, improve the quality of communications and increase trust levels. You may, of course, have to sell the idea to your boss (the first test of managing upwards)!

Such meetings should certainly be short, but they must be regular (for example fortnightly). You should also make sure there are no interruptions (it takes twice as long to get back on track) and that you limit the time spent on each agenda item.

Yes, I know you will argue that you have too many meetings, but the quality of these meetings will be such that it will negate the need for other meetings and will create the influence you need to get on and get things done. It can give you the inside perspective on your boss's agenda and priorities, clarify any misunderstandings and improve the general quality of the relationship.

Rather than passively trying to work out your boss's priorities, or getting frustrated by lack of contact, you must take a large part of the responsibility for managing the relationship. Then you will begin to influence upwards, to your benefit, to the benefit of your function and, even to the benefit of your boss!

LINK TO YOUR PEOPLE (1): RELATIONSHIPS

How are you doing as a leader? The answer is, how are the people you lead doing? Do they learn? Do they take the initiative? Are they growing and developing? Are they getting promoted? Do they want to get out of bed in the morning? Do they want to work for you? Do they go the extra mile?

When you retire, you won't remember (or be remembered for) how well you did in the first quarter, or how much money you saved the organisation. What you'll remember (and be remembered for) is how many people you developed, how many people you helped have a better working life because of your interest and your active involvement in their development. If you ever need to question how you're doing as a leader (and I recommend you do so frequently), then find out how the people you lead are doing; then you'll really know.

Let People Know Where They Fit In

Even if we are all cogs in the great corporate machine, it is often good to relate how important each cog is. By explaining to individuals where their job fits in and the value it adds to the organisation, they will feel valued and important. Because they are!

Seeking out one individual and taking them through where their own particular contribution actually fits into a project or task can make them feel special and give them a context for their efforts. Otherwise they can feel like automatons, working in isolation with no connection to the rest of the business.

So take responsibility for finding out how the efforts of each of your staff fit into the grand scale, and tell them. Raise the visibility of those performing lower-impact roles (especially among those who are performing high-impact roles). Include all staff in project meetings so that all can feel part of the team and understand where their part fits into the whole. Explicate in concrete terms, with examples of how good performance affects you, the team, the department and the organisation.

Where to Expend Your Energy

15 %   70 %   15 %

As we saw earlier, most organisations have around 15 per cent so-called "movers and shakers", i.e. individuals who will take the initiative, embrace change, and act as a positive influence. At the other end we find 15 per cent cynics. In the middle we have the critical mass who will move in the direction of whichever group is in the ascendancy. So, it is better to focus our energies, not on the cynics, but on those at the front end who can pull those in the middle along. Indeed, the theory is that if we sacked all the cynics, then 15 per cent of the others would become cynical and so drop into the left-hand box!

Identifying and nurturing those who are positive will have a positive impact on the organisation. Consider how you are currently identifying and nurturing talent. Who could be your future successor(s)? What are you doing about it?

You Don't Have To Like All Staff Equally, but You Must Treat Them Equally

As with life in general, we all find we like some people better than others. The key is to get the best out of all individuals who report to you, and this means getting to know what makes them tick. What are their values? What motivates them? Why do they come to work? What do they like and dislike doing? What are their dreams and aspirations?

To get the best out of your people, you need to have the answers to these questions; otherwise you are administering rather than leading your team. People are complex, but not unknowable. Taking the time out to understand all your staff will make you a better leader.

Discuss your own performance with an employee: What could you do differently? What more could you do to help? How does your managerial style impact that person, the department, the business? Be brave and be prepared to hear bad news; development starts with the truth.

Meet regularly with each of your team to discuss how their development plans are shaping up and generally how they are performing. This will get each of them into good habits, give them a focus for their development and help maintain momentum.

Identify career "aiming points" for individuals. Determine with the individual where this point is and agree what needs to happen to support them. It is OK to tell an employee where you see them going and developing, and how you might help them get there.

For those employees who will be moving "up" the organisation, this task is quite easy. Work with them to agree an "aiming point" where *they* want to get to, where *you* think they are capable of getting to.

Discussing the Difficult Topics

Where leaders often fight shy is speaking with those employees whose careers might have plateaued, who are unlikely, or don't want, to get any higher. I have worked with so many leaders who have found this to be like discussing body odour, and simply ignore the subject, pretend that it doesn't exist! Yet it leaves many employees, usually longer-serving staff, feeling abandoned and uncared-for. Developing upwards in the organisation (vertical loading) is the easy bit. Developing those who have reached their peak (horizontal loading) is more difficult.

The first hurdle is to sit down with the individual and find out how they are doing. I have known many cases where the employee sees it as blessed relief that they won't have to go for promotion, and that they won't get fired for saying so! Then it is a question of broadening them. Putting them in charge of a couple of new recruits to mentor them during the first crucial year. OK, so after a year the new recruits will move onwards and upwards, but it means that they will still be providing a valuable role to the organisation. Broadening the remit, giving extra responsibilities, all develop individuals without the pressure of trying to climb the leadership pyramid, which, as we all know, gets steadily narrower the further we climb!

Try to catch people doing something right — and tell them! How often do we tell people when they have dome something wrong. Well, how about telling them when they have done something right. And further still, proactively looking for them doing something right so that you can tell them!

Another way of getting in close is to gain an understanding of your staff's workload. Do you really know how much they actually have to do and how long it takes them to complete?

The Black Spot

If I draw a tiny black spot in the middle of a white board and ask a manager what he sees, the answer is always "a black spot". Very few managers ever say, "an immense expanse of white with a tiny black spot in the middle". Yet there is far more white space than black spot! This is an excellent example of getting a manager to focus on the fact that it is too easy to see the one bad thing someone has done (a mistake made, something forgotten), ignoring all the good things they do day in and day out.

From Command and Control to Support

The numbers of direct reports we often have means that it is not possible to dictate, control or monitor. So the only way to manage is to trust, to let people make their own decisions. The framework within which we can do this is our values, which create a common set of shared beliefs and ensures the decisions our direct reports take will be within this framework. It is the role of all leaders to create this value framework to support the central organisational ethos.

Don't lecture — simply state your point-of-view. The concept of "leader as teacher" is not to lecture, but to nurture, support, guide and develop.

It is too easy to accept issues at face value. Yet how often are our perceptions in life wrong? It is the same with leadership; we need constantly to question our understanding, our perceptions and our motives. In issues of conflict, look for "layering"; that is, under-lying issues which may be the real cause of strife. Then have the courage to bring these up with the individual. Although the issue is often one of lack of time, it is essential to buy that time to look beyond the stated reasons, to get to the real issues as to why staff are unhappy, or why someone is not performing. A quick fix or "banging heads together" does not usually create a lasting solution.

Remember, "the right message at the wrong time is the wrong message".

Give criticism tactfully and never in public.

Sometimes it is necessary to, as they say, "develop individuals *outside* the organisation". This is not a clever, funny euphemism for sacking folk or treating them lightly. Your staff deserve to be treated with dignity and respect. However, this does not mean you should allow staff to fail. After confronting poor performance early, talking with the person and agreeing a plan of action to address the problem areas, things often perk up.

Yet sometimes we find someone who continually under-performs, even after coaching, cajoling, nurturing, development and a great deal of time and patience. It is the leader's responsibility to ensure that people perform and to continually allow an individual to fail means that you as a leader are failing. So it's OK to manage someone out of the business, help them get fixed up in a job, in an organisation, where they will succeed. Many leaders I have known fight shy of this option. But poor performance must be confronted and dealt with immediately. Habitual poor performers can affect the morale and performance of the rest of your team. If you can put your hand on your heart and say you have tried every angle, taken advice, done all you can, then maybe you need to openly and honestly plan an exit for the person.

Involving Others

Proactively look to involve your team in your thoughts and your decisions. Until they feel they can experiment and do things for themselves, they will need to look to you for guidance.

Teach them good habits. Like Pavlov's dogs, if you solve the problems, whenever there is a problem, the bell rings and they come to you for "feeding".

Visibility

Increase your visibility. "Facilitative style" management has often led managers to feel (and be) remote from people and therefore out of touch with what is going on. We need to walk the walk, support people, ask what more we could do to help.

When situations get a bit fraught, I am frequently surprised how much staff want and value a manager's direct intervention, clear direction and sound leadership — even down to being told what to do. We need to get out of our chairs, talk to people, energise and focus them, support them. Perhaps we ought to focus less on helping staff "cope" with issues and more on getting them to think for themselves and develop for themselves new and better ways of doing things.

We should demonstrate passion, for our people, for our values, for our business and for our customers. As we discussed earlier, we cannot change our basic personalities, but we can modify our behaviour. So by demonstrating passion, I do not mean behave unnaturally, or wear a false nose and a twirly bow-tie, if this does not fit with us as a person. What I am saying is, in our own ways, ones that are most comfortable for us, we should show everyone we really care about what happens.

Why is it that some managers still have offices? Just a thought.

Interaction

As I outlined earlier, behaviour is interactive (even if we would often prefer to say that it isn't!), and our behaviour will determine how another person behaves towards us. It is also, to go further, important for us to recognise the impact of another person's behaviour on us. How we "respond to" or "react against" the behaviour of another person is yet another measure of us as leaders. We will at times almost need to force ourselves to "respond" rather than "react", allowing the other person to see a measured, rational perspective, even in (especially in) emotionally charged or difficult situations. A considered response, open questions and placing the onus back upon the other person will help take the prickle out of such situations. "Reaction" is exclusive and can alienate, whilst "response" is inclusive. Here are some real life examples:

The other person exhibits forthright opinions without providing examples or rationale:

> "These production deadlines are unachievable."

Or even the more personal,

> "Why do you always set such impossible deadlines?"

You could *react* by saying:

> "Well, if you can't keep up . . ."

You could *respond* by saying:

> "OK, take me through your rationale."

Or, in the latter case:

> "I thought we had all agreed the deadlines, but let's look again at them."

The other person begins to drag the conversation away from the original point:

> " . . . But the staff are unhappy anyway; do you remember the time when . . . ?"

You could *react* by saying:

> "That's got nothing to do with it."

You could *respond* by saying:

> "I'm unclear how that fits into what we're discussing."

The meeting is being dominated by two strong characters, to the exclusion of the others:

You could *react* by saying:

> "Be quiet!"

You could *respond* by saying:

> "OK let's see what everyone else thinks. What about you, Julie?"

Several participants are expressing their views at the same time:

You could *react* by saying:

> "Cut the noise, I'm in charge."

You could *respond* by saying:

> "Right, we now have several ideas for discussing; let's go through them one at a time."

You feel that someone has a negative reaction but may be concealing it:

You could *react* by saying:

> "Have you got a problem with that?"

You could *respond* by saying:

"Take me through your thoughts on this."

Try not to use words like "problem" (almost a label), and be careful of your use of the word "why", which if said in certain ways can sound punitive. If you say, "Why?", it can be very provocative, whereas using the phrase, "Why do you think that might be?" can be a gentler and more effective way of getting someone to open up.

I have worked with many leaders who display, at times deliberately for effect, "designer anger". This is where someone comes into the office with a problem, the boss launches a tirade against them, the person leaves suitably chastised, and the boss returns to a conversation with me smiling and not in the least bit angry or perturbed. I used to find this when I worked in education, where I would be having a quiet, interesting conversation with a teacher in the staff room and suddenly, out of the corner of her eye, she would espy one of her pupils waiting to talk to her. "What on earth do you think you are doing bothering me during break times? Get off to your lesson this instant and I will speak with you later!" Our conversation would resume in the same quiet manner and at the exact point where we had been.

One argument I have heard for this phenomenon is that, as it is only designer anger, the person has chosen to behave in this way and so it is a response rather than a reaction. Yet this takes no account of the impact it has on the other person, nor of the "model" the leader is providing to others in the organisation. Also, what will you do when you *really do* get angry?

Informal Networks

All organisations have informal networks, developed over time to supplement (and in many cases, by-pass!) the existing formal channels. These can serve a variety of purposes: to share information, to share resources, to solve problems, to generate ideas, to gain influence, etc. Much of the day-to-day work within organisations happens through these informal networks. In actual fact, to disregard these informal networks, or to doubt their existence, can make your job more difficult and certainly more frustrating. Often, the only way we can experience the informal network is by seeing those who are not part of it feeling "left out", or distanced from others. This can cause delays in information coming back, or blockages in trying to get new initiatives pushed through.

LINK TO YOUR PEOPLE (2): ENCOURAGING CREATIVITY AND RESPONSIBILITY

Thinking Contextually

Organisational life is hard enough without having to think about extra things. Yet, by thinking more broadly than our own remit, we can develop a greater understanding of issues and be better placed to make more timely and effective decisions.

An issue, any issue, does not occur in a vacuum. It has a context. So to understand an issue fully, we need to examine the complex relationships surrounding the issue, and "map" them.

This means literally drawing the problem in a box and then a series of boxes either side of this to highlight the relationship and interdependence with, and on, other issues. This will help you to place the issue in context, upstream and downstream.

Involve others in this to bring them in, and make sure they are clear on what you are doing. This will raise your profile as a decision-maker and help your staff understand the process of contextual thinking.

Thinking Upstream and Downstream

The late Robert Goizueta, CEO of Coca-Cola, asked a question of his senior managers: "What is our market share?"

"Forty-five per cent," came the confident reply.

"How many ounces of liquid does a human being need to drink a day?" Goizueta asked.

"Sixty-four ounces a day," came the puzzled reply.

"On average, how many ounces of all of our products does a person drink per day?"

"Two ounces," came the response.

"What is our market share?"

With that idea, Goizueta changed the future of a 100-year-old institution. Coca-Cola had assumed, by the way they calculated market share, that the market was saturated. Goizueta pointed out that their competition was not Pepsi, but *any other beverage*.

Reflect on the concept that Goizueta is expounding. How could the concept provide a different perspective on how you, and your people, think about some of the issues affecting your function?

Read the chapter on "Systems Thinking" in Peter Senge's book, *The Fifth Discipline*. Then look at some of the issues in your own function, "upstream" and "downstream".

Passing Some of Your Tasks "Down the Line"

At appraisal time, proactively look to pass 10 or 15 per cent of your current activities "down the line" to your direct reports. This will focus you more on "the bigger picture" and offer your staff the opportunity to further develop. I know the idea of being forced to give up a part of your job sounds procedural, almost punitive. But it does get leaders into good habits. Getting leaders into good habits can be just as difficult, but by making it mandatory that 10–15 per cent of the leader's role is "handed down" at appraisal time, after a while it will become just like brushing your teeth.

Act as a role model — let individuals see how you do things and solicit feedback. Ask each individual what more they need from you. If you really consider that your staff are watching you with a view to how to behave as a leader (or even as a person) then it will focus your mind on your own behaviour! Rather than wonder if staff are watching you — encourage them to!

One of the most frustrating aspects of delegation is where a manager delegates an activity and then, when the direct report comes back and says how difficult it is, the manager feels they have to take it back. Delegation in this respect is like a heavy box. It has to be completely given up and, when the direct report comes back, help them find better ways of carrying the box. But don't take it back!

Encourage Ideas

Create a culture in which ideas and suggestions are actively encouraged, at first through departmental meetings and then as routine. Even if we are out until 2.00 a.m., we still brush our teeth, no matter how tired we are. This is simply getting us into good habits.

Similarly, good habits can be instilled in all of us and by actively encouraging staff to come up with ideas (even if it is uncomfortable for them at first), then the habit will be created and reinforced. But remember, first efforts may lack some polish!

Getting staff to the point where they feel comfortable in "outing" ideas will require a process of listening to and encouraging ideas that are not going to enhance the business. It is easy, out of short-term expediency, to simply come up with the ideas yourself, rather than let staff take a long time to come up with an idea which is not as good as yours. However, if you truly are in leadership "for the long haul", and really want to leave behind a legacy, when you move onwards and upwards, of radical, conceptual, fresh, thinking individuals, then you will have to accept some early disasters. I bet even Van Gogh's early works were such that only his mother loved them!

Let your team see something of you as a person, i.e. open up on your fears, your dreams, etc. If you starve people of information, they will make something up to fill the void. This "something" will be determined by how they feel about themselves, so just give a little bit more, and try to make this across the board with each and every member of your team.

Stretch Objectives

Include stretch objectives as part of your staff development. For example, set interim tasks which fall outside their usual day-to-day work, ask them to give feedback to the senior team, let them lead a team meeting. "Stretch" objectives are those which "stretch" staff and where there is a potential for failure. Most staff are unlikely to fail in the basic tasks which form part of the role. Many objectives that are set have no real difficulties or "danger" element to them. We learn best from experience, failure and the threat of failure. So, if you really want to develop your people, really push them on, agree some stretch objectives and watch their muscles grow!

Remember to thank people!

The "Negative" Room

Take time out every so often to allow your team to have a whinge session. This means dumping all the build-up of negatives in one go. One way of doing this is to designate one part of your meeting room as "the negative arena", for an hour, half a day, a day. Let people physically move to that part of the room during the session to speak out negative thoughts or post negative messages. In the rest of the room, everything must remain positive.

This situation creates the conditions for a "safe" environment in which everyone (including you!) can let off steam about anything that isn't going well or is wrong within your department or function.

Once the issues have been brought out into the open, they can then be transferred to the positive side of the room to be worked on and addressed.

Unstructured Problem-solving Sessions

Try to break the structured approach by having unstructured problem-solving sessions with your staff. This will bond the team, boost morale as well as get things changed for the better. Having a structured, prepared session can end up being an opportunity to simply air all that is wrong with the business, function or department. Also, by saying "what is wrong", our brains head straight for the negative issues. If the focus instead is "how can we make things better" then the spiral becomes a positive one, rather than negative. So a semi-spontaneous session where you take your team and ask one question, say "what would make things better for our customers", and then brainstorm a response. This will also get your team used to "free-fall", i.e. speaking out ideas without worrying about how it might be received. You will know they are being successful when your staff begin to hold such sessions even when you are not there!

Being Politically Aware

The Americans call being politically aware "savvy", which comes from the French verb *savoir*, "to know or be aware of". Knowing and being aware means taking certain things into consideration; it does not mean being subservient.

Using sound political judgement is an important characteristic of managers within all organisations and, as such, it should be developed and nurtured like all other characteristics. You may want to call it politics, but I would rather call it "influence".

Taking the time to reflect, to "read the runes", will make you better placed to make correctly timed decisions, and know when to wait, when to make your move, when to back off. Once again, your method of developing "savvy", developing diplomatic judgement and awareness, will come through understanding yourself and others and spending time reflecting on past situations where you have "lost".

Also, watching "good operators" (and poor ones!) will help you see how others achieve what they want. Don't fall into the trap of trying to be like someone else, just use the information to help you reflect on the sorts of things you should be doing differently to achieve what you, and your team, need to achieve.

Influence can mean getting results through individuals, or teams, over whom you have no direct control or management "clout". Rather than saying, "well, I've done my bit, now it's up to them", consider how you might influence their actions. This is a measure of senior management.

Weigh up the Benefits of Fighting the Battle

Carefully consider your battles before you fight them. If you go for a "win", what will it do to your relationship with the loser? If you are viewed as stubborn, this may harm future perceptions on particular issues. Try to establish in advance how others will respond to your agenda. You should spend more time preparing before any major discussions — be clear on your message and your important issues.

Monitor any tendency you may have to get to a win only situation. Look for positions proposed by others which you could live with and agree to do so.

The Parable of the Snake and Frog

In his book, *The Greatest Management Principle in the World*, Michael LeBoeuf recounts the old parable of the snake and the frog. This is where a fisherman stumbled upon a snake sitting with a frog. Feeling sorry for the frog, he picked it up and carried it to safety. Feeling sorry then for the hungry snake, he gave it a shot of whisky from his hip-flask. Next day the fisherman returned to the same spot to find the snake waiting for him — with two frogs! And the moral of the tale is: *you get what you reward*.

So what does your organisation reward? What do you as a manager reward? Do you reward efficiency or effectiveness, initiative or mindless conformity? Do you reward simplicity or needless complication, seniority or added value?

Answering some of these questions will help you understand the culture of your organisation, the impact of your own leadership and the behaviour of the people you lead.

What do you think you should be rewarding in future?

LINK TO YOUR TEAM

A team can achieve what no individual can. Understanding teamworking and team dynamics will enhance our capabilities as a leader. We should know the motivations, capabilities and limitations of those in our own team. The need to understand individuals is, in my opinion, paramount in leadership. However, this needs to be extended so that we understand how teams operate and the value they can add to projects and the business in general.

Therefore we should read about teams, learn and understand team dynamics, team goals, the benefits of teams and how to utilise teams properly in problem-solving.

This will allow us constantly to analyse, reflect and provide feedback on how well the team is working together. We should therefore also teach our team about teams so that in discussions we are all talking the same language and all have the same level of understanding.

Diversity in Teams

Read *Management Teams: Why they Succeed of Fail* by R. Meredith Belbin. Belbin's early work emphasised the need for balance in successful teams. This is often difficult for managers to grasp, as they often seek to "clone" (i.e. build teams in their own image). Yet Belbin showed that even building "super teams", which he called "Apollo teams", does not create the conditions for successful teamwork. The "Apollo teams", made up of the most intelligent, most confident, most outspoken and articulate individuals, fared poorly both in competition with other teams and in projects within industry. Indeed, "Apollo teams" did less well even than those teams comprising the meekest, under-confident, underachieving individuals.

The reason is that these "Apollo teams" were made up of individuals who were the product of an education system where coming first was of paramount importance. No one would concede a point, no one waited to listen to the views of the others; they spent endless time in abortive debate and arguing minor points and no one wanted to take notes! Successful teams need a balance, and so we should celebrate diversity, rather than look for clones.

Team Definitions

A true team must have specific results for which the team is collectively responsible, and the performance ethic of the organisation must demand results. So, unless you have a common purpose and clear goals, you are not a team; you are simply a collection of individuals. Coming together as a group of people does not make you a team. How you work, how balanced you are and what you achieve will. So, rather than say "the management team", for the collection of individuals who are managers, focus on what it is that makes you a team. Are you really a team?

The One Minute Manager Builds High Performing Teams by Kenneth Blanchard is a simple, powerful book which will provide you with an excellent basis for understanding, building and managing any team. In it, he compares the attitudes of two construction workers performing the same task. When asked what they are doing, one says that he is trying to crack a piece of granite; the other says he is part of a team building a cathedral. This shows the importance of creating a sense of vision for your team.

Process Mapping

Arrange for your team to be taught (or better still, you teach them) process mapping and project planning so that they can better present their ideas and to get them into the habit of measuring. Process mapping is easy; it is not an exact science or part of the mystique of consultants.

Laying out the total processes of your organisation, all the things that are done, your business, or your function, in blocks so that areas of duplication and triplication are clearly highlighted is not difficult and it will get you and your team working together on an issue which is an integral part of your working lives. And if you mess it up, so what?

The Real Extrovert vs Introvert

So much psychological terminology has seeped into our day-to-day language and, as it does so, often takes on a new, "populist" meaning. Extrovert and introvert are two such terms. They are often seen as "outgoing, popular, party animal" versus "boring, unpopular stay-at-home". This is not, of course, what Jung meant when he coined the terms. What Jung was describing was "where we draw our energy and focus our attention". Extroverts tend to draw their energies from, and focus on, the external world and will typically, "do, reflect and do". Introverts, on the other hand, will draw their energies from, and focus on, the internal world and will typically, "reflect, do and reflect". Now there is a question of the extent to which each of us is an extrovert or an introvert. Many of us, even if we fall on the side of being an extrovert, will need to take time out to reflect and re-energise. However, the distinction is still useful, because it provides a framework for understanding why individuals behave in the way that they do and, more importantly, how best to influence them.

For example, an extrovert will prefer to communicate by talking, including explicating their ideas whilst they are formulating (speaking it out as they think about them). An extrovert will also learn best through doing or discussing and focus more broadly and in less depth.

An introvert will prefer to be reflective, communicate in writing or one-to-one and work out their ideas by reflecting on and then verbalising them. Introverts will learn best by reflection, will be private and self-contained, more comfortable with silence and will tend to focus on a narrower range of interests but in greater depth.

So what does all of this mean in the world of organisations and teams? Well, if you were trying to sell something to another person (a product, service or an idea), then knowing whether the person is an extrovert or introvert would help. Selling to an introvert, we would need lots of examples, details, testimonies, be prepared to leave literature or details with the person and accept they will need time and space to reflect before making a decision. To sell to an extrovert, it is better to verbalise, to speak of the benefits, to get them deciding quickly.

Similarly, if you are leading a team, knowing which side of the extrovert/introvert divide that each team member is on will make it easier to motivate them, develop them and apportion tasks. An extrovert will tend to like participating in a variety of tasks, and can become impatient with jobs that are long, slow and intricate. They may also act quickly, without thinking through all the implications, become easily diverted (especially by people, conversations, phone calls, etc.) and will like having people around.

An introvert will, conversely, tend to prefer quiet private space, be happy to work on the more detailed single project over a longer period of time and without interruptions. They may find phone calls or other diversions annoying and will prefer to develop ideas alone and through reflection.

The point here is not to put everyone into a "box", but to provide some sort of backdrop through which we can all find out more about the people we lead (and ourselves!). As suggested earlier, our people are the raw materials, and the more we know, the better we will be able to lead them. Also, such models as Myers Briggs Type Indicator (which uses the extrovert versus introvert scale) are useful as starting points for getting to understand others fully. Once we have isolated some characteristics, then we can go much further. Rather than saying, "this person is an introvert" (our starting point) we build a relationship and move to "this introvert is a person". Leadership is about people, not models. And the models should be the beginning of a journey towards complete understanding, rather than a box into which we place all our staff and colleagues.

LINK TO YOUR CUSTOMERS

Change, in all organisations, is far more effective and lasting when the breadth, depth, frequency and consistency of customer contact is high. There is also a very high correlation between the amount of executive customer contact and the speed of organisational change. A closer relationship with our customers also helps keep competitors at bay; gets our customers acting as advocates for us by telling others how good we are to do business with; and makes our transactions less price-sensitive — people are always happy to pay for service — and more relational.

Customer service is far too important to be left to customer service departments. So, other than making the odd visit with the salesperson, what can we, as managers, do to connect more fully with customers?

All managers and executives within the company should personally handle a proportion of customer complaints. This will expose them to the "sharp end", and provide an opportunity to see how difficult it is dealing with such problems. Imagine what a signal this will send around the business and to the customers! Also, personally addressing these complaints will often mean having to work across several departments to provide the solutions and so offer each manager a wider business perspective than their own function.

Each manager, especially in the service sectors like finance and human resources, should have apportioned to them a discrete set of key accounts so that each can get genuinely "close" to a few customers and "own" them.

Thus each manager can conduct "customer mapping", i.e. get to know a different set of influencers and decision-makers within our customer's organisation, and build, maintain and enhance relationships.

When the apportioning of key accounts to each manager is seen to be successful, why not have all managers tasked with income generation from these accounts? Question: who is responsible for sales within the organisation? Answer: we all are!

Customer Information

I'd like to see managers become obsessed about the need to be informed in general, and to want to acquire better customer information in particular. Not for its own sake, but to improve the business and design "seamless" processes.

Customers are in a unique position, looking in from the outside, and experiencing the organisation's behaviours and processes on a regular basis. Imagine utilising this information to recreate process and behavioural alignment, continuously improving our businesses with the customer as the driving force for change. They also love to be involved.

I would argue that an out-of-touch leader is probably not a real "leader" at all. We should drink in information, and our customer information should be seen as important as our financial data. Collecting and sharing this information will make a significant difference to our business, and how we do business.

I am not talking about sending out questionnaires. Sending out customer questionnaires simply confirms the fact that we are not close enough to our customers in the first place. Why don't I send my friends questionnaires? Because I know what they think of me, as I have an ongoing relationship with them.

So when we are connecting with our customers, at our place or theirs, we should ask lots of questions about their business, where it is changing, what the future is, etc. We should also be asking what they think of our company, what we should start doing which we currently are not, and what we should stop doing which we currently are, and record and share all this invaluable information.

Also, look at how our current processes and behaviours add value (or not) to our customers and use this information back at base to begin to change things and bring the business into line with our customers. If we understand their processes and behaviours, then we can modify our own.

Don't make assumptions about service, keep the dialogue ongoing. I always pride myself on ensuring our company provides the best service possible to our customers. Yet I had a shockingly good learning experience with one of our major customers who has been involved with us for many years and whom we know (or thought we knew) intimately. Whenever I visit their offices in London, whatever we agree, I get back in the evening, write up the notes/type the report/put together my conclusions and fax them back to my customer first thing in the morning.

Perfect service, right? Wrong! When I went out for a beer with my main contact, he explained how annoying it was that I left his office, went back to base, and fired off the report to be on his desk the next morning, before he arrived. He told me it made him feel inadequate, that he began to feel that he should be working later and getting in earlier, etc. My assumption that every customer will want things done quickly took no account of how it made him feel. I never bothered to ask!

So, in my desire to provide "excellent" service, I was actually failing miserably, because "excellent service" can only be defined by the customer, and only at a specific moment in time. In other words, defining "excellent service" can only be done by the customer, and this definition must be constantly reviewed. It's not easy, is it?

The Customer-centred Leader — The Direct Report as Customer

Imagine your direct reports being able to change their supplier. "Hey, I'm sorry, but the leadership service you are offering us just does not come up to standard! All our complaints have fallen on deaf ears, you have not listened or changed your ways and so we are terminating our relationship." Scary thought, isn't it?

Staff often have leaders foisted on them; it is not a democratic process. Yet we speak so often of the concept of the internal customer that this has become standard (if a little outdated) organisational parlance. So imagine your staff did have the "opt out" clause; wouldn't it change the way you interacted with them?

As organisations become more customer-focused, it is easy to see the customer as the person who buys the product or service, or even as those within other areas of the business to whom we link in "the value chain". But hasn't the leader a duty to provide a service to their direct reports?

Do we understand what they need? Are we providing them with the right level of service? If we accept that the ultimate arbiter of all of us as leaders is the people we lead, then how do we truly know whether we are being the kind of leader that they need to lead them and bring out the best in them? Remember, how we measure the performance of our leaders will determine how they behave. And for "our leaders" we can say "ourselves". If we are measured only on functional expertise and functional outputs, then that is how we will behave. So it is not enough to say that we ought to be more people focused (if that is what is important). We need to ensure that we measure our leaders against the criteria we determine as important. Then we can ensure we develop good habits.

LINK TO COMMUNICATION

Listening

Listen! We need to listen (remember, not pretend to listen but really listen) to what all the people say, and keep connected to all the people all the time.

We should record and act on all information that is given to us, and remove all obstacles that hinder excellent performance from our people. The people know what needs to change and be made better, so we need to listen and help them act on it.

We should also set up planned connections, take staff out to meet customers, suppliers, competitors, design houses — widen everyone's world, broaden their perspectives. We need to open doors, horizons, worlds even. Staff, at all levels, should be asked to take visitors and customers around on company tours. If this means extra development for them in order to feel comfortable doing this, then great! Then capture this data and use it to improve. There is little point having customers in, or taking staff out to meet suppliers, simply as a social activity. Question and listen, and generate information which will make you better at what you do. External sources are such a "mine" of information and should be fully utilised.

Listen for the whole message. This means going beyond hearing the minutiae, the words and the facts that the speaker communicates. As you process all of the information (this involves listening!), try to understand the bigger picture. Do this by listening for the main thoughts and ideas. Try to view these thoughts and comments from the speaker's perspective: why does he or she think the way he or she does?

Practise non-verbal attending. This achieves some important objectives: It sets a comfortable tone, encourages the other person to talk, demonstrates interest and concern, signals that you are listening. Non-verbal attending involves keeping eye contact, occasional nods. Prepare for distractions before you meet the individual. This may mean disconnecting the phone, closing the door, etc.

Listen without interrupting. Don't start to speak before the other person has finished talking. Over the next couple of months, mentally record the number of times that you:

1. End someone else's sentence;

2. Butt in.

3. Interrupt the flow of someone's conversation.

If you do interrupt, are you sitting forward in your chair when you do it? You are far less likely to interrupt when you are relaxed and leaning back.

Take time to respond to what the other person is saying. Respond and don't react. Be aware of any tendencies you have to daydream or let your thoughts wander. This reflects poorly on you, so don't do it. Keep eye contact. And use open questioning techniques.

Open Questioning Techniques

Open-ended questions begin with who, what, how, where, etc. You can never answer yes or no to an open question. They also allow the other person the freedom to talk, and are especially helpful if you are prone to responding too quickly, or when you are likely to give a rapid opinion to either defend yourself or prove the speaker wrong. This type of situation usually leads to a win/lose situation: you win, they lose.

Open questions also allow the person the opportunity to speak, giving their thoughts, feelings, and maybe even ideas. Look at this example:

"Communication is a real problem in this company."
"In what way?"
"You never talk to me."
"How can we improve our communication?"

You automatically place the onus on the other person to respond. You have more time then to process information, measure your response, and also build a relationship with the other person by listening to them. You demonstrate value when you choose to listen.

Begin to practise open questions with friends, and this will demonstrate how they work. Also, try playing the question game with a friend, which involves beginning and perpetuating a conversation by only asking questions, allowing for a short pause to think (around two seconds or so). For example:

A. *"Did you know it is raining outside?"*
B. *"Do you have windows in your office?"*
A. *"The rest of the building has windows, doesn't it?"*
B. *"Do I spend all my time searching for windows?"*
A. *"What do you spend your time doing?"*
Etc.

This is an excellent device for stimulating rapid lateral thinking, and working on the development of probing responses to direct questions.

Practise Response, Not Reaction

Recognising the difference between response and reaction will help you to lead away from an emotionally charged exchange or situation. How you respond will help to determine the final outcome, either negative or positive. Facilitate discussion in order to get to a better understanding. This will give you more time and more information before making a measured decision or giving a considered answer.

Also, make sure you don't become the king or queen of the e-mail. It is so easy, especially within larger organisations, to send e-mails to cover yourself or with political intent, all hidden under the umbrella of communication. Sending an e-mail means you have sent an e-mail; it does not necessarily mean you have communicated. Communications are received, not given. Therefore, if the other person did not receive the message, then you have not communicated. Taking responsibility like this may help you to think through what you are communicating and to whom. Also, how many people would simply send e-mails if the "confirmation of having been sent" notice was omitted? Communication is a desire to tell people something, and it is up to you to choose the best medium. E-mail is a wonderful tool, but if it negates taking a cup of coffee up to someone's desk and saying, "Can I have a word?", then it can be a curse rather than a blessing.

Conveying a Sense of Urgency

It is important for leaders to convey a sense of urgency. The trick is that this must be at the most appropriate times. Convey no sense of urgency and you probably won't get people achieving on time. Convey urgency in everything and your staff will begin to question your motives. "If everything is urgent, then nothing must be urgent and so I will develop one speed."

So a sense of realism in what really is priority and what can wait, will help in motivating your staff when they need to be. Defining "urgent" is also useful. Does it mean "drop everything else"? Does it mean it needs to be done now, even if we have to work over-time? So, use real language and tell people when something needs to be done, why it needs to be done, by when it needs to be done, and where it fits into all their other priorities. Then they will under-stand what *you* mean by "urgent".

LINK TO VISION AND STRATEGY

Understand the endgame and share it with everyone. I don't personally like clichéd mission statements. However, all the more successful organisations with which I have worked tend to have a clear vision of where they intend to go and what their values are. What is required is our own "magnetic north", a clear direction against which the rest of the organisation may be redefined.

Create a compelling story for the future to galva-nise your team. This is almost a, "We get out of bed in the morning and work hard because . . ." type of statement or, "What are we like?" People don't gen-erally remember figures or details, so make it "real" for people. "In three years' time we will look like this, our customers will be these type of people, our shape will be like this, etc." Make it interesting and memorable.

Storytelling is also easy to pass on and, whilst it may gain some slight alterations along the way, it will be more likely to be passed on and permit every single person be clear as to where the future lies, and exactly what the magnetic north looks like.

Creating such a vision is a communication challenge, rather than a design challenge, so that everyone is on the same page. We also need to reinforce the vision at all opportunities and be seen ourselves to live it. If we say that our organisation is a fun place, then we can't be seen to be miserable and scratchy. If we say we are committed to teamwork, then anyone walking around should see teams in action everywhere and find no evidence of the cult of the individual. (Perhaps we shouldn't even find evidence of individual bonuses!)

All the people in our organisations should be able to, as they say in the US, "give the elevator talk". Imagine someone gets in the lift with you and says, "what is your organisation all about?" In the time it takes to travel two floors, you, or any of your staff, at all levels, should be able to paint a clear and lucid picture of your business, its purpose and values, what it does, how it does it, what it is like to work there, and how the future is shaping up. Could you do this?

A Zero-Based Approach

Try a "zero-based" approach. Get your team(s) together and ask the question, "If we had no systems or
structures currently in place and had to create them
from scratch, what would we do?" You then have a
greenfield site with which to work. This exercise allows everyone an input into improvement and leads
away from rutted thinking and the approach that,
"things have always been done this way". It will also
help integrate teams and create interlinked processes. Behave like an external consultant to your own
business or function. This will help dispel the "we
tried this before in 1980" syndrome, which can be the
assassin of change.

Sand, Buckets and Stones

Imagine an empty bucket, which you have to fill with
a number of stones. The stones are of various sizes
and shapes ranging from large rocks to tiny pebbles.
The tendency is to start with the smaller stones. Yet it
is only by starting with the larger stones, and *putting
these in first* that all the others will fit around them.

This is like putting together a strategic plan. Most
groups of managers start with the small issues and
get hung up on these. By identifying the bigger
"stones", the really important issues that need to be
addressed, the smaller ones will naturally follow. It is
often useful to actually draw a bucket, draw the
stones, formally name the "big stones" and then let
your staff "fill the bucket" with the smaller issues.

Scenario Planning

Get your team together and imagine it is exactly two years from now. Write the date down. Then, firstly, imagine the department is closing down after a dreadful two years. As a team, determine where it all went wrong. Look back two years: What was it like? Where did the seeds of decline come from? How did it begin? Who was to blame? Write the whole scenario down.

This will help you see, *and feel*, what it could be like if everything went wrong without actually going through the real pain.

Now go back to the future, but this time a successful future. What went right? What is the shape of the business? Who are your customers, how do you serve them? What did you, as a team, do right? What did you stop doing? What did you start doing? What did you change? How does it feel?

This exercise gives you the power of hindsight and can lead to your strategic plan for the business/function by focusing on difficult issues but in the safe environment of the future. Strategic plans, for functions, departments and organisations, need more than facts and figures. They need to be *sensory*, i.e. using the five senses. History began as a series of colourful stories handed down by word of mouth, with clear descriptions, pictures, names, faces, etc. Creating a strategic plan, which all staff can feel part of, needs the same kind of flavour, the same breadth, the anecdotal feel of an interesting story and an all-encompassing picture of how the future looks, and where people fit in. Then everyone can embrace the "vision". Steer clear of mission statements, objectives and tactics and begin with a clear, interesting, imagination-capturing picture of the future. And if it doesn't fire you up, then how can you expect it to fire anyone else up?

LINK TO CHANGE

As we discovered in Part One, most of us only like change when it means "changing things"; when we realise it might involve changing our own behaviour, we quickly backtrack and rationalise reasons *not* to change. Managers are often the guiltiest parties. Remember the distinction between buying and being sold to?

Before you talk about how change is inevitable and how we must all accept new ways of doing things, consider how this may be received. People are far more likely to support and feel comfortable with change if they have an input into the process. There are many reasons why people resist anything new and understanding these will enhance your performance as a leader. Below, I examine all of these factors and suggest some steps to "ease" the change process for yourself and for your organisation.

The "Loss of Control" Factor

It is said that "power corrupts"; yet, within organisations, it seems that "powerlessness corrupts", as people seek to hold onto the past, possibly a halcyon past which never really existed but is now worth fighting for as it is better than the unknown. When individuals (that is, you and I) feel powerless, we can become "rule-bound" and petty and try to keep hold of some tiny piece of our world that we can control, and then we proceed to control it to death. If people feel involved, they feel they have some control, and if they feel they have some control then they are buying, rather than being sold to. Then you can harness the energy in a positive way and engender commitment, rather than resistance, to the "cause". Therefore the first step in the change process is: *Involve people in the process.*

The "Uncertainty" Factor

If people don't know where the next step is going to take them, then it is the organisational equivalent of walking the plank. Anything new seems dangerous and so may well be resisted. By not informing staff what is happening, why and when, allowing them into the process, we encounter resistance. The change process is essentially an information issue. "How do you eat an elephant?" The answer is, of course, "one chunk at a time". When eating the elephant of change, it is important to the success of the process to divide the whole process into "bite-sized" chunks, a number of smaller steps, rather than a huge leap of faith. People can then focus upon one step at a time, they know where each step leads and they can look backwards to see where they have been, so the whole process seems logical. The second step is: *Create and publish a step-by-step plan with milestones.*

The "Surprise" Factor

We can all be shocked by decisions that are sprung on us without any groundwork or preparation. The first natural reaction, when we have had no time to mentally prepare, is resistance. Waiting until all the decisions have been made and then springing them on staff can mean they have no time to assimilate and consider what might be positive in the "new order".

In *The Fifth Discipline,* Peter Senge uses "the parable of the boiled frog" to describe the process of adapting to challenges and threats, rather than avoiding them. He compares it to the difference between placing a frog in a pot of boiling water and placing him in a pot of cool water and gradually raising the temperature until he boils. So, managing the expectations of staff is essential. The third step is: *Give advanced warning so people can get used to the new ways.*

The "We Got It Wrong" Factor

Often, in recognising the need to change the way things are done, we underestimate the feeling of "everything we've ever done was wrong" which can lead to people feeling foolish or, worse still, wanting to defend the old ways. Hurting pride can create a cause or a crusade for individuals. Past actions need to be seen in context, to the extent of acceptance that some things might have been right for their time, but now we must move on. People often need the opportunity to grieve before letting go of the past. Often, this can mean pinning up a history of past events and achievements on the notice board, or having a formal "wake" or a celebration and cutting off of the past before moving on. The crucial issue here is to ensure that those who we want to move forward have sufficiently let go of the past. So, the fourth step is: *Hold a formal wake!*

The "Extra Work" Factor

An area of resistance to new measures comes from those who see it as "extra work". This was brought out most clearly during the "quality revolution" of the 1980s, when many organisations were determined to achieve ISO 9000 simply to compete and get on the tender list. Many saw adhering to a quality system as extra work rather than "*the* work".

Doing things differently, even for all the right reasons, can take more energy, more potential for failure and greater mental exertion. People can find plenty of reasons to resist new ways if they don't want to make the extra effort. Step five is: *Reward those who are going the extra mile.*

The "Past Resentment" Factor

Grudges may be terrible things, but they do exist and will begin to come out during times of change, times when strange things are happening, breaking the old patterns and requiring new approaches and extra effort. Every whinge and grudge will surface and can escalate into a deluge of negativity against the new ways. These may not take a direct confrontational tack but may be a conspiracy of silence, hampering efforts to get things moving.

Sometimes it is necessary, before we can move on, to go back and encourage grievances to surface earlier, deal with them and close them out before getting back on track. Therefore step six is: *Allow some negative sessions.*

The "Real Threat" Factor

Sometimes when new paths have to be trodden, we do, unfortunately, create "winners" and "losers". Part of the process of managing our responses to change is recognising the realities of its effects and honestly dealing with them. It is essential to avoid false promises or pretence, especially playing "the glad game". If there are going to be losses, people should hear about it sooner, rather than later; otherwise their fears may affect others. This can make those we may want to keep, those with "get up and go" to "get up and go" . . . to some other organisation. Also, for many, the truth can be an unburdening. Once our worst fears have surfaced, we can focus on the solutions, rather than conjecture and gossip. For managers, the recognition that resistance to change is not irrational, but is a normal response, may be difficult. Yet this recognition is essential. If the manager can harness this energy and fear, and turn it to the advantage of the company and the individual, then the whole process will be smoother and the new ways adopted much more quickly. Therefore, step seven is: *Give it to them straight.*

Communicate Change

If there do have to be major changes, rather than simply *saying* that things will need to change, it is important to include three essential elements:

♦ *The case for change.* A clear statement of why things can't go on the way they have been.

♦ *Where we are going.* Creating and articulating the picture of the better future, using picture form and all five senses. As with creating a vision of the future, people learn best when they hear a story, rather than get bombarded with figures and facts.

♦ *How we will get there.* What will your people, as individuals and a team, have to do (and stop doing) to create this future?

A Bit of Controversy

Maybe we should all, as leaders, encourage controversy. Good leadership, in my experience, makes allowance for well-intentioned failure. The so-called "quality revolution" and the search for "zero defects" can negate risk, so maybe we should be more forthright with our people and encourage risk-taking, rewarding those who try but fail. We could work with our people, agree what needs to be different and then say, "What do we need to do or to change to make this happen?"

The more radical the goal, the greater the impetus for change. "Removing the safety net" often works: "OK, you have been complaining that things are not right, you lot come up with solutions." The easy part of any business issue is identifying the problems; the hard part is determining what we should do about it. This is not simply radical for the sake of being radical, but an attempt to break with the incremental improvement school. It may have a place, but it may negate quantum leaps. Whenever I hear of incremental steps of improvement, I am reminded of the old childhood lateral-thinking puzzle of the frog leaping across a pond in ever-decreasing steps, so that he never actually makes it all the way (see Part One). This is also my concern over the incremental, "small steps" school of business improvement. Where will your giant leaps come from?

We need to be careful of *kaizen*, or setting up a continuous improvement process, as this can often negate a quantum leap, or an inspirational idea, as it focuses upon smaller chunks of incremental change.

Rutted Thinking

Rutted thinking" is the enemy of change, of improving the lot of your staff, your colleagues, your organisation, yourself! Take time out to look at issues from different angles, different perspectives.

At staff meetings, put a couple of blockages to improvement on the table and get your team to act as consultants to your own function, department or organisation. Imagining that you have no history, no previous involvement can be an excellent way of seeing stale or difficult issues in a fresh light, from a variety of perspectives. This process will lead to improvements and greater effectiveness, but it will also help build and bond your team (without mentioning the dreaded word "teambuilding"!), create a unifying, common purpose, get them thinking "out of the box", and energise them as they are achieving.

LINK TO IMPROVEMENT

Create a desire to improve. We need to improve *ourselves*. We need to read, we need to think about things — lots. As William Blake said, "The man who never alters his opinions is like standing water, and breeds reptiles of the mind." To prevent the reptiles of the mind, we need to constantly review our thinking and move away from the "we tried that in 1980" syndrome which destroys radical initiatives.

When we watch the film *The Greatest Story Ever Told*, it tells us very little about life in Biblical times. However, it tells us a great deal about Hollywood in the 1940s, and how the film industry viewed Biblical times. In the same way, every work of art is essentially a product of its own time.

Think of a great album, say, *Sgt. Pepper's Lonely Hearts Club Band*, or *Band on the Run*, or *Ziggy Stardust*, or *What's The Story, Morning Glory*. They are all products of their time. And times change. Because an idea did not work, or was viewed as not worthy at one time in the history of an organisation, it does not prevent it from being valid now.

Improving Ourselves

We need to widen our own worlds if we are to develop ourselves and others. In the same way as we need to understand ourselves before understanding others, we need to begin the continuous process of improving ourselves before we can improve other people or other things.

Improving Our Organisations

Organisations, like people, are like some other organisations, all other organisations and no other organisations. This is why you must establish your own values. Not a wish-list mission statement, which could feasibly be hung on the walls of an engineering company, a doctor's surgery and the local supermarket. I mean spending half a day saying what you really are about as an organisation.

Sometimes we can achieve this by brainstorming the ten things that we really hate. Then, the opposite list becomes, de facto, our values. This does not need to take a long time — in fact, the less time the better.

Get your creative forces together, establish a zero-based approach (but don't take aeons over it!), and don't be a copycat — at least not yet. You may find that, by doing so, you have lowered your standards, and negated a great deal of potential.

Improve Our Processes

Process improvement teams, involving folk from all areas and levels of the business, are useful for effecting continuous, positive change. The group leader should plan for and initiate early wins, i.e. identifying issues which will have a major impact on the business or function but which can be quickly and relatively easily achieved. Maybe get a senior manager to sit on the team (and therefore attend every meeting) but don't let them lead it. Invite customers to participate. Improvements should be in all areas and celebrated — loudly.

Any process improvement team should look at behaviours as well as processes, as true service excellence and continuous improvement align processes and behaviours.

Improving Workflow

Process improvement is not as complex as it sounds. Indeed, the simpler the process improvement, the more effective it tends to be.

Draw a simple diagram of the current layout of your section. Map workflow and travel patterns, who walks where, who interfaces with whom, etc. Then look at the positioning of workstations, files, desks, machines, etc. Does it all make sense in terms of efficiency and effectiveness? Is the geography conducive to better communications and ensuring that those who need to work together are placed close together?

You are the manager; you can make the necessary changes to improve the lot of your staff and the effectiveness of your function. Don't complain about your lot — change it!

Qualitative Measurement

Create qualitative measurement criteria. If we accept that relationships with staff, with customers, with other departments are so crucial for the development of the business, then we should measure these relationships, these so-called "softer" issues. In all the analysis we have undertaken, it is the "softer" issues that are the "hardest" to measure and yet, paradoxically, these are the ones against which our customers judge us. Customers tend not to articulate it very well but, in their minds, this is how we are judged.

When we ask our customers' customers how they measure the performance of their suppliers, they usually say "accuracy of order and on-time delivery". Yet when we point out that a particular supplier often delivers late and that the order is often incomplete or inaccurate, they smile and say, "Well, we like them." It is this "like" which we need to truly understand and make sense of if we are to enhance our service levels.

We could bring customers in on staff appraisals, ask suppliers what they think (and use these comments in appraisals) and get other departments to comment on our performance as a department. This is not to say we are initiating TQM, which is simply a label and may even be seen as extra work. What I am saying here is that if we are serious about improving and developing, we need proactively to solicit meaningful information from all sources who experience our behaviours and processes on an ongoing basis, and record and use this information to improve, and be seen to be improving.

We *can* audit knowledge. If we constantly question, open people up, get them telling us what they know, we can build up a known stock of intellectual capital. If this sounds jargonistic, imagine devising a questionnaire for our staff which records their qualifications, their out-of-hours activities, their interests, their views, their extra-curricular skills, etc., etc. Consider how much better we would know them and how much better we could utilise these skills and knowledge and how much richer their working lives would be by bringing the basics of genuine outside interests into the workplace. This could also widen the whole concept of how we develop staff, developing to enrich lives and so create a happier, better read and more broad-based workforce.

It also helps remove some of the mystique surrounding people. How often I have heard a manager say of someone, "He has no get-up-and-go." Then we discover he is captain of the local pot-holing club and is involved in paragliding!

The "80/20" Rule

The "80/20 rule" tells us that 80 per cent of the value of a group of items is generally concentrated in only 20 per cent of the items. Therefore, by using the "80/20 rule", you will be 80 per cent effective by achieving 20 per cent of your goals (*the most important* 20 per cent). So, if you have a "to-do" list of 20 items, you will generally be 80 per cent effective by successfully completing only the four most important items on the list.

LINK TO LEARNING

"Training", as I said earlier, is a passive term, something that is "done to us". The active terms are "development" and "learning", which will happen after training or indeed in the absence of training. These terms will keep us moving forward, keep us curious. This requires a major movement of mindset and an acceptance that we never really "get there". There is no single point at which we could arrive and say, "I have learned", as learning is a journey, not a destination. It is a way of life.

Learning is also about choice, rather than ability. Contrary to the popular saying, we can also see old dogs learn new tricks. The key is not "teaching" new tricks, but encouraging the willingness to learn. Being a leader who is continually learning and developing is also an excellent signal to send to staff and others in the organisation.

Just as parents have a major determining influence on the behaviour of their children, so leaders have a similar impact on the behaviour of the people they lead. This is a responsibility many of us may seek to deny.

The Americans have an expression called "modelling the way". This means acting as a role model for employees and setting an example of excellence. If you want an energetic workforce, then you need to be seen to be energetic. If you state that you want a happy workforce, you cannot then behave in a miserable way. If you want staff to get things done on time, and meet targets, then you must do the same. Leaders often forget the influence, good or bad, they have over their staff. Good habits, integrity, honesty are all contagious. So say one thing, and do it.

The Words Manager and Educator are Synonymous

The acid test for all of us as leaders is not whether we can take decisive action and make smart decisions today, but whether we can teach others to be leaders and build an organisation which is even more successful when we are no longer there. The organisations that win most often are the ones whose leaders invest the time and energy to develop lots of leaders. For great leaders, teaching is not an occasional activity; it is at the heart of everything they do.

The Competency Matrix

Look at the *Competency Matrix* model on the next page. In our learning and development processes, we move from unconscious incompetence (area 1), to conscious incompetence (area 2). This is a significant movement forward in our learning, as we realise our shortcomings and areas for development. Becoming "conscious" also allows us to move from conscious incompetence to conscious competence (area 3). Then comes the real learning curve, as we move from conscious competence to unconscious competence (from "knowledge" to "know-how"). This is where our learning and development becomes habit, it becomes "just the way we do things".

Holding the "mirror" up to individuals and to organisations can bring about a realisation of *where* things need to change. This is not really so difficult. Moving from one phase to the next (i.e. determining *what needs to be done* to improve things), is slightly more difficult. But the real gain is the transitional, "unconscious" move into the unconscious competence area. This is where the learning and the behaviours become habit.

Getting into the right habits takes time, and it takes transition through the four areas. Many managers reach area 3 and believe they have "learned", they have arrived at knowledge. Yet only when it becomes habit, unconscious, day-in, day-out, even under pressure, can we say it is know-how.

4. Unconscious Competence	3. Conscious Competence
1. Unconscious Incompetence	2. Conscious Incompetence

A Basic Law of Biology: L ≥ C

"For any organism to survive, its rate of learning must be at least equal to, or greater than, the rate of change in its environment."

For the word "organism", we could substitute "organisation", or even "individual"!

For years, Pete Sampras was the world's number one tennis player. Yet he still kept on being coached and developing, day after day, week after week. It is not enough to say, "I don't have time to learn." The world is changing fast and we all have to move quickly just to keep pace. The alternative is clear from our law of biology.

Question, think, listen, reflect, act. The best leaders also seem to be the best teachers *and* the best learners.

Sacred Hoops

In the book *Sacred Hoops*, Coach Phil Jackson talks about his time working with Michael Jordan. Jordan was so gifted a player that Jackson could not offer him anything which might improve his basketball play. So he set about transforming a basketball player into the team leader. Jordan began to see his role, not just as scoring baskets, but to help raise the ability and potential of the whole team. It was this that helped turn the Chicago Bulls into the unbeatable team they were. One lesson which football teaches us is that great players don't always make great coaches or managers. It is one thing to be able to do something but quite another to be able to explain it and pass it on to others.

Maintaining the Status Quo

If you don't see the advantages of promoting learning and development amongst your people, you probably won't buy in, and things will continue to happen as they have always happened. So consider the present without the encouragement of continual learning.

Short-term fix instead of long-term solution, the same mistakes, excuses and frustrations perpetuated, overly dependent staff, lack of initiative, questions without answers, an exodus of your best people, frustrated creativity, missed opportunity, people who maintain the status quo and resist change, performance within capability, running hard without reward, no time for development . . . etc. Do some of these ring true?

LINK TO THE WHOLE PERSON

As we have seen, people are complex and strange, with all of our little foibles and idiosyncrasies. Henry Ford said, "Why is it I get a whole person when all I want is a pair of hands?" To be truly successful, today's manager *needs* "the whole person" with all of their strengths, foibles, idiosyncrasies, passions, highs and lows; and managers need to understand and make sense of these in order to manage. This is the main challenge to managers and yet is the one most easily shied away from.

Such acceptance may also be too radical and lead us away from the quick-fix "management skills" menus and box-ticking mentality which reduces "management" to a series of easy-to-learn steps, like Bert Weedon's "Play in a Day" guitar course, or Enid Blyton's "Noddy Becomes a Leader". This fundamentally goes against my own experience and beliefs. Managers, all of us, need to take responsibility for our own learning and development and not assume that what worked for one aged trainer will work for us (if it ever really worked for the aged trainer).

Bring me the man who gave him those scars

I hear too many people talking about having the "scars of experience on their backs". In the film *The Magnificent Seven*, Yul Brynner is seeking desperadoes to defend the town. One of his young colleagues finds a man whose face is badly scarred and suggests he be recruited to the team. One of the other members of the gang says, "No, bring me the man who gave him those scars!"

The point I am making here is that the scars themselves mean nothing; it is what we learn from them and how we have developed and modified our behaviour since that counts. Indeed, too many scars may mean, as in the case of *The Magnificent Seven*, that there has been no progression, no movement forward or developing strategies to defend against attack, and this is why the scars keep appearing.

Tom Peters, in his book *The Pursuit of Wow!*, quotes an American football coach who says it's not his job to motivate people, it is his job to remove obstacles to prevent people becoming de-motivated. In my view, he is doing 50 per cent of his job. Imagine what the coach could achieve if he really got in there, used his experience, got his hands dirty and really supported his people and fired them up. That's where we should be heading. Leadership is about getting involved. Not doing work for staff, but helping them develop, learn, and take on new responsibilities. Enriching their working lives so that they want to get out of bed in the mornings. If this sounds altruistic, well it is. But from a purely commercial standpoint, a motivated workforce is a productive workforce.

The Encouraging Summation at the End!

I hope you have found this book thought-provoking, interesting, funny and, most of all, helpful. I hope it strikes a chord with you. It seems to me that the concepts are stuff our grannies know! Sometimes mentioning the unmentionable can be seen as a bit radical. But we have all seen the outputs from the "management skills training" solution. Exactly! The ideas within the book are not so much concepts as practical common sense, based on my experience of working with lots and lots of leaders.

This book is about you. Yes, I know how cheesy that sounds, but the key is that you can modify your behaviour, you can become much better at what you get paid for and you can develop (and continue to develop) the unique leader in each of you. We all can, if we choose. It is too easy, especially with so much on our plates, so many priorities, so little time, to take the "I'll book myself on the 'skills' course" route. The choice is yours, of course, but I hope you will now give that some serious consideration, along with the alternatives I have described throughout the book. The key is to get to the pitch where development, like teaching, does not become extra work, it becomes *the* work, just the way you do things and live your life.

You remember in the early 1970s there were posters declaring, "Today is the first day of the rest of my life"? No, I didn't like them either. However, there is an important parallel here. Don't look backwards, look forward. The past can suck us backwards if we let it and prevent us from becoming the leader we are capable of being, of achieving our potential. Accept who you are — you're alright. Then begin the process of understanding the impact of your behaviour, and then begin to modify this in the light of your new understanding. You will be amazed at how far you can go.

Frankenstein Is the Doctor, Not the Monster

Forget the "Frankenstein" idea, that we can create a "perfect" leader. However, we *can* achieve great things. What we can achieve is to know ourselves, understand other people and, in the light of this understanding, to continually modify our behaviour and become constantly and continuously better at what we do, leading other people.

It is interesting that, when I ask groups of leaders to draw Frankenstein, the results bear a close resemblance (whatever their artistic ability) to the features portrayed by Lon Chaney Jr in the original film. Very few grasp the fact that Frankenstein was the doctor, not the monster. The point here for all of us to learn is that we are in control of our destinies in terms of the kinds of leaders we want to be. Only we can create the leader, or the monster, in us.

Try to artificially graft on the stale regurgitated ideas of trainers on "skills-based" training courses and you may find the townsfolk, torches in hand, beating a path to your office door, crying, "Death to the monster." Alternatively, push outwards, get to know you and learn to bring out the great things that are in there. Find the missing links, begin to re-connect and amaze yourself.

If you want to enter the "monster" debate about training and development, or take the ideas contained within *Frankenstein's Manager* further, then you are invited to visit our website:

www.prelude-team.com/frankenstein

Recommended Reading

Senge, Peter (1993), *The Fifth Discipline*, **Century Business, 1997 Reprint**

A difficult book and certainly not one to be read before you go to sleep. Senge drowns us in detail and theories together, drawing on examples and people with whom he has worked to try to get "the formula". I just don't accept the notion of a formula. Indeed, he even brought out *The Fifth Discipline Fieldbook* to help us with the more practical elements, but this was still a bit like a guru preaching to the unwashed. However, there are some gems, well hidden, waiting to be discovered in terms of "the leader as designer", "systems thinking", and "shared vision". If you don't have time to read all 424 pages, then read pages 17–92 and you will get the message.

Tom Peters (1995), *The Pursuit of Wow*, **Macmillan**

Almost a book of tabloid headlines with no rational argument or back-up data. But this is probably why it works. It is almost a stream of consciousness, without structure or detail, like one of his lectures: breathless, witty, draining, insightful and annoying. There are some wonderful moments, but some boring half-hours. This is the sort of book which should be read in one fell swoop, say on the plane or train, and then thrown away. Its lack of structure and form is probably why it works so well. Worthwhile for the little things that stick in the mind afterwards.

Stephen R. Covey (1990), *The Seven Habits of Highly Effective People*, Fireside Books (1999 reprint Simon and Schuster)

Although I do not hold with Covey's "seven habits", this book can nevertheless be useful in getting us thinking about our own habits, how we are "known" by them and the impact of them. I love the idea of getting leaders into good habits, but where I would disagree with Covey is that I do not believe there is a definitive set of habits to be universally applied. But as a stimulus for encouraging us to think more broadly about attitude and behaviour, and establishing our own habits, behaviours and values, it is worth the money.

Eugene Pascal (1994), *Jung to Live By*, Souvenir Press
Isabel Briggs Myers and Peter B. Myers (1993), *Gifts Differing: Understanding Personality Types*, Oxford Psychologists Press

Both of these books offer us a structured understanding of the differences in people. It is often argued that we must refrain from putting people in boxes, but I disagree. It is only by placing different "types" in different boxes that we can begin to see the rich tapestry of life, in that people come in all sorts of shapes and sizes, metaphorically speaking. Once we understand that we must manage diversity, then we can release people from the boxes by recognising their own unique personality. But if we are to study people, we must start with some sort of framework and both of these books are excellent starting points.

Eric Berne (1970), *The Games People Play*, Penguin
Thomas A. Harris (1995), *I'm OK, You're OK*, Revised Edition, Arrow

These books are primarily about Transactional Analysis, and this is a superb way of getting us to concede that behaviour is actually choice and that the way we behave will determine how other people behaves towards us. It offers a simple model of Parent, Adult and Child and focuses on truly understanding what is at play when two or more people interact. The language may be a bit "groovy 1960s academia", but the message is useful for all managers.

Charles Handy (1995), *The Empty Raincoat*, Arrow

Charles Handy has a quiet wisdom, and this is probably his best work. I know everyone talks about *The Gods of Management*, etc., but I reckon he came up with a couple of gems in this book. The Sigmoid Curve is a mindset mover, the simplest model for change you will ever see, and can be used at individual, team, functional and organisational level. The great thing about the Sigmoid Curve is that, once we have taken it on board (and every person I have shown it to has done so), then it carries with it a certain responsibility to actually gauge where we are on the Curve and do something about it.

Ricardo Semler (1994), *Maverick*, Arrow

This is an inspirational book about how to change mindsets, how to buck an outmoded system and how we really can be radical in our business design. Semler provides many useful examples of how he went about completely changing the organisation to be sensitive, responsive and more profitable. He has followed this book up with some inspirational seminars in the UK, challenging leaders to put their radicalism where their caution is and really change things, rather than prop up a rotten system by mere tinkering. The only credibility problem with Semler's incredible passion, ideas and drive for change is that he owned the organisation. Many leaders I have met have used this as the "get-out clause" for saying, "Well it is alright for him, he owns the company!"

Adrian J. Slywotsky and David J. Morrison (1998), *The Profit Zone*, John Wiley and Sons Ltd.

An excellent book for getting us focused on profit, as opposed to turnover, market share, etc. The authors use simple, straightforward models to make their

points and most leaders can identify their own organisations in these. Indeed, in organisations that
cannot find "their model", I have used this as the basis for determining their own unique model. Like
many books in the genre, however, the large chunk
of text at the end is devoted to examining the usual
US corporations and a glimpse at Jack Welch's diary.
I would recommend you read pages 3–70 and this
will be all you need to begin to take a long hard look
at your own business, whatever the size.

Eliyahu M. Goldratt and Jeff Cox (1993), *The Goal*, Gower

This is an old favourite, as it makes some excellent
points about how businesses run and why people fail,
all within the bounds of a novel. This makes it easier
to identify with, as there is actually, if not a hero, then
a central character. I have often recommended it to
manufacturing people as a way of getting them to
stop banging their heads against a brick bottleneck
and look up.

Ken Blanchard (1993), *The One Minute Manager Builds High Performance Teams*, HarperCollins

Blanchard uses the "Situational Leadership" model
(outlined in Paul Hersey's book *Situational Leadership*), to make the case for outlining phases of team
development. Although many other authors have
spoken of "team phases", Blanchard goes further and
outlines the role of the team leader in influencing the
team; from complete control at the initial stage,

(*"Why are we here?"* *"What are we trying to achieve?"*), through to total freedom for the team, where the leader acts more as a consultant. This is a simple, effective way of explaining why teams are not working and, more importantly, what you can do about it.

Roger Fisher and William Ury (1993), *Getting to Yes*, Revised Edition, Arrow

Fisher and Ury take the tack that negotiation does not have to about "winners and losers". It is possible, indeed desirable, for everyone to leave the negotiation table believing it has been a good deal. This may sound like a new age, pseudo-philanthropic tract, until we realise that these guys negotiated at world "super-power" level. There is also an excellent supplement, *The Negotiating Style Profile* by Rollin Glaser and Christine Glaser, for those interested in measuring their negotiation style against the Fisher and Ury model.

Jon R. Katzenbach and Douglas K. Smith (1998), *The Wisdom of Teams*, McGraw-Hill

Although this is a long book, it does provide a good rationale for why building teams is important. It also offers some good models of definition for teams. Not inspiring, but good examples and lots of knowledge to equip us to better understand and teach our teams.

R. Meredith Belbin (1996), *Management Teams: Why They Succeed or Fail*, Butterworth-Heinemann

This was the first real book on teams that was backed up by research and was user-friendly (even before the term "user-friendly" was coined). If you are interested in well-researched but more difficult and brain-stretching works on teams, then Wilfred Bion's *Experiences in Groups* and *Learning From Experience* will provide the sort of challenge you are seeking. Belbin's book was the first to look in-depth at the need for balance in a team, and demonstrate that "Apollo Teams" (those made up from the more confident, bright and outspoken individuals — much like the old idea of "think tanks") perform badly, indeed worse than teams made up of less bright and under-confident individuals.

Michael LeBoeuf (1987), *The Greatest Management Principle in the World*, Berkley Publishing

The anecdote about the frog and the snake is used to good effect by LeBoeuf to get us to the excellent conclusion that "you get what you reward". I have used this many times to establish organisational or departmental culture, and I believe we can learn so much about organisations by determining what it is they reward. I take this further by emphasising that if the organisation rewards mindless conformity, then it cannot expect radicalism. Conversely, if an organisation does reward radicalism, then will it reward spectacular failure and mistakes (by-products of radicalism)? LeBoeuf's book is only 123 pages, but is still over-long. The idea he espouses is a good one. However, like Covey, he then tells us what he thinks we should be rewarding. The book works, if we can read it, take on board the idea, and then question ourselves. However, when it takes us through the ten strategies we should be rewarding, then I switch off.

Index